66

591

ALE

EASTERN
FELLS
50.-63

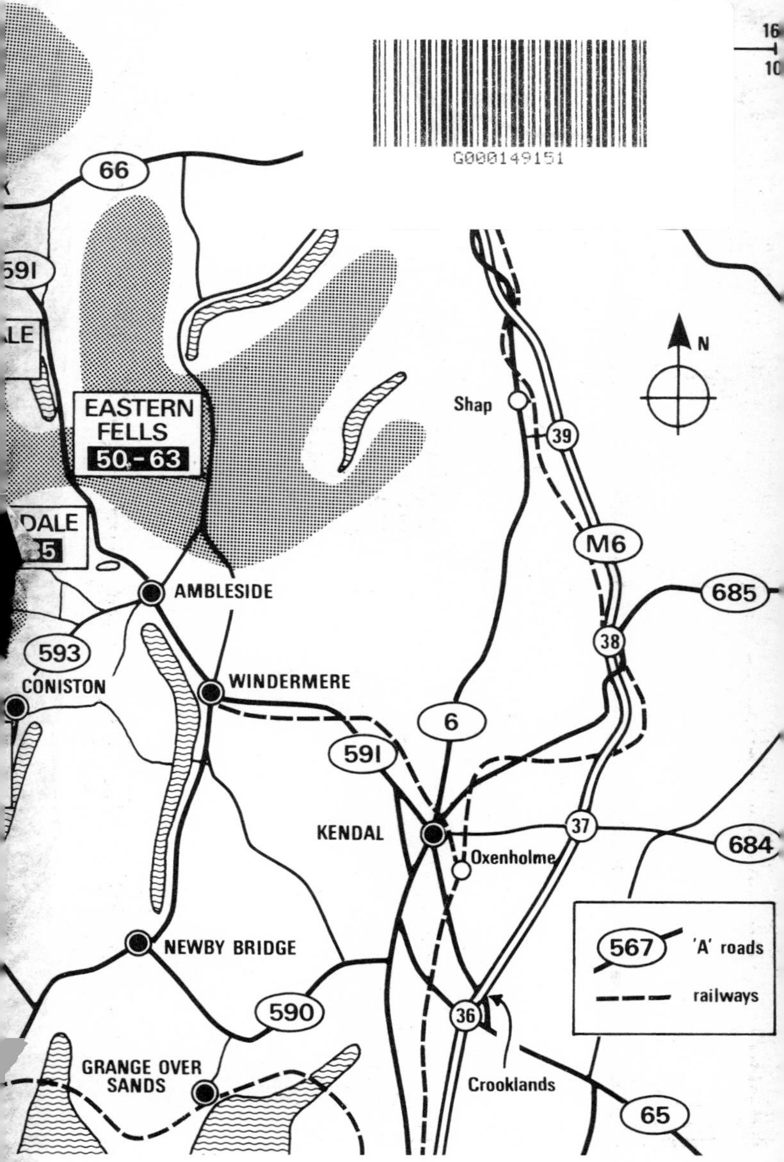

DALE
5

593
CONISTON

AMBLESIDE

WINDERMERE

Shap

39

M6

685

38

6

591

KENDAL

Oxenholme

37

684

NEWBY BRIDGE

590

36

Crooklands

65

GRANGE OVER
SANDS

N

567 'A' roads
- - - railways

G000149151

100 CLASSIC CLIMBS

LAKE DISTRICT

Stephen Reid and Steve Ashton

The Crowood Press

First published in 1989 by
The Crowood Press Ltd
Ramsbury, Marlborough
Wiltshire SN8 2HR

This impression 1992

British Library Cataloguing in Publication Data

Reid, Stephen
    100 classic climbs in the Lake District
    1. Cumbria, Lake District, Mountains –
    Visitor's guides
    I. Title II. Ashton, Steve, *1954*-
    914.27'804858

ISBN 1 85223 055 X

Acknowledgements

A gratifying number of people lent their support by suggesting climbs for this book.
Many also went out of their way to assist with route checking. Others have helped with
the diagrams or historical information. I owe them all my profound thanks: Martin
Armitage, Frank Booth, Tim Carter, Ian Conway, Iain Clark, Sid Cross, Colin Downer,
Harold Drasdo, Dennis English, Muriel Files, Rick Graham, Tony Greenbank, Harry
Griffin, Andy Hall, Neville Hannaby, 'A. B.' Hargreaves, Glynn and Alistair Hopkins,
Andy Hyslop, Dave Kay, Les Kendall, Dave Miller, Dave Mitchell, Mick Nunwick, Geoff
Oliver, Walter Phipps, Keith Phizaklea, Alan Rowntree, Nigel Sale of the National
Trust, Dave Seddon, Luke Steer, Andy Tilney, Oliver Turnbull, Ivan Waller, Alexa
Wightman, Charlie Wilson and Bill Young.
    In addition I would like to thank the Fell and Rock Climbing Club (F&RCC) of the
English Lake District for so kindly allowing me the use of its excellent library, journals
and guidebooks. June Parker, the F&RCC librarian, has also greatly assisted by
checking historical accuracy.
    Lastly, but most importantly, my long-suffering family. Jilly, Euan and Ingram (not
forgetting Bunyip) – may you finally realise who that strange man so besotted with
barometer and wordprocessor really is.

Front cover: Needle Ridge, Great Gable (Route 18a).
Back cover: Scafell Crag in winter.
(Photos: Stephen Reid.)
Frontispiece: Napes Needle, Great Gable (Route 17).
(Climber: Stephen Reid. Photo: Steve Ashton.)

Disc conversion by Columns Typesetters of Reading
Printed in Great Britain by Richard Clay Ltd, Bungay, Suffolk

Contents

Preface

This guide selects classic rock and ice climbs from the Lake District and describes them in a new way. Topo diagrams take the place of formal route descriptions, while an accompanying text provides supplementary information.

Strictly speaking, the title *100 Classic Climbs* is inaccurate. In many instances a number of routes have been clustered under one heading, and in fact over 170 climbs are fully described with further information provided on winter routes.

The book is the result of collaboration between Steve Ashton and myself along fairly strict lines of demarcation. Basically I am to blame for the choice of routes, the essays and so on, whilst Steve has produced the finished artwork from my rough sketches.

Whilst many people have made suggestions regarding the selection of routes, the final choice remains my own and they can in no way be held responsible for it. In any case, about 70 of these routes picked themselves. I doubt if many climbers would question the inclusion of New West, Central Buttress, Napes Needle or other routes of comparable status. Of the remainder, the gullies (as summer rock climbs) have a lot to offer in wet weather and are 'good for the soul' in a hair shirt sort of way. The Lake District is not as reliable a winter climbing ground as Scotland (or even Wales), and so the selection of winter routes is a compromise between what is good and what is likely to be in condition. Another aim was to include a full day's climbing on each crag, though this has not always been met. Finally, a few climbs owe their place to personal favouritism — not surprising considering I have included only routes that I have climbed myself.

Grading was another factor in the selection of routes. Upper limits were set at E2 and, in winter, IV/V. Most climbers starting out today should be able to climb at these standards at some time in their career. Thus there is no reason why, with determination, a regular visitor to the area should not aspire to ascend every route in this book. In doing so you will be privileged to discover much of the best that Lakeland has to offer.

S.J.H.R. 1988

Climbing in the Lake District

Lakeland is arranged like a spoked wheel with the valleys radiating out from a hub at the aptly named Great End on the north-east spur of Scafell Pike. An absence of roads over this central area allows each dale – and the crags within – to retain its own distinctive atmosphere. Thus there are climbs here for all tastes: from short roadside desperates in Borrowdale to long mountain climbs on Pike's; from serious routes on Scafell's East Face to classic Napes ridges; from an easy walk-in to Dow to an all-day expedition to Scrubby; and from the brilliant rock of Gimmer to the shattered flakes of Buckstone How. The choice is yours.

Comparisons between climbing in the Lake District and in Snowdonia are invidious but inevitable. The Wales-based climber who said that he liked the Lake District 'because the fishing is so good' showed the typical tongue-in-cheek bias of the incorrigible partisan. As one who has lived for long periods in both areas I can honestly say, without contradiction, that whilst the climbs may be better in North Wales, the climbing is best in the Lakes. True we have no Tremadoc, no Gogarth, no Cloggy (though Scafell comes very close to the latter), but there is a lot more to climbing than good rock. The Lakes possess a beauty that is unsurpassed throughout the length and breadth of Britain. A beauty that has inspired generations of poets and artists – Coleridge, Wordsworth, the Heaton Coopers, Banner, Wainwright. A beauty that never fails to take one's breath away, however often one may be privileged to view it. A beauty that lifts these small climbs into a sublime realm.

I offer no excuses for dwelling on the history of Lakeland climbing in many of the accompanying essays. My only regret is that there was not room to tell more of it. Times may have changed since the days when Botterill gallantly raised his hat, or Holland, falling from the Scafell Girdle, proudly remembered to shout 'God Save the King', but we still climb for much the same reasons. When they pioneered these routes they too were young and yearning for adventure. In knowing their story we can appreciate a little more about the climbing in this beautiful district and also, perhaps, about ourselves.

There are no hills
  like the Wasdale hills,
When spring comes up the dale.

George Basterfield, 'Wild Cumberland',
    from *Songs of a Cragsman* (1935)

How to use the Guide

AREA INTRODUCTIONS

Routes are described under one of eight area headings: Wasdale, Ennerdale, Buttermere, Borrowdale, Eastern Fells, Langdale, Eskdale and Southern Fells. A brief introduction to each describes climbing typical of the area and highlights major crags. Further notes identify approaches by car or public transport and suggest where to look for accommodation. An accompanying map locates valley bases, parking places, and crag approach paths.

ROUTE INFORMATION

Concise details of each route are presented under six headings:

Summary: A short appraisal of the route for quick reference purposes. Along with route grade and length, this tells you all you need to know when looking for ideas.

First Ascent: Brief historical details (first names have been included where known).

Best Conditions: Helps you find a suitable route according to the season and prevailing weather.

Approach: Gets you to the crag with a minimum of fuss. Provides concise information on parking, as well as on the approach route and its duration (times given are for a fit Englishman who does not stop to admire the view, draw breath or otherwise procrastinate. Competent Scottish pairs, with an infallible faith in Clough's Ben Nevis guide, will probably expect to halve these times). Grid references refer to the relevant Ordnance Survey map. If you have trouble remembering in which order the figures are used, think of positioning a ladder against a wall: first move it *across* – then climb *up* it – not the other way around!

Starting Point: In the first Lakeland climbing guide, Owen Glynne Jones wrote, 'Place a man at the right starting point, and he will easily find the upward line of least resistance, though not so swiftly as he would trace out the downward line if he slipped.' With the former aim in mind, starting points have been described with great care. Further assistance can be gained from studying the topos and crag diagrams.

Descent: Briefly describes the most common descent routes. These are often included on the crag diagrams as well.

ROUTE DESCRIPTIONS

The essays following the summarised route information are designed to whet the appetite whilst in an armchair rather than help with route finding on the crag. However, there may be the occasional clue secreted here!

TOPO DIAGRAMS

For simplicity, all routes are identified by a number from 1 to 100 (subdivided alphabetically where required). These numbers are used consistently throughout the text as well as on topos, crag diagrams and area maps.

Topos take the place of formal route descriptions; you will be surprised how quickly you learn to 'read' the route by interpreting these symbols. A key at the rear of the book explains what they mean.

Most topos have either been drawn whilst climbing or been based on photographs, so relative distances between stances and other features should be reasonably accurate. But don't read too much into each little twist of the dotted line. Topos can only show the approximate line of a route; it is also necessary to use your own good judgement.

Some topos serve clusters of two or three routes. Numbering and lettering makes it plain which is which. In some cases a worthwhile neighbouring route has also been indicated.

GRADINGS

Normal adjectival grades, suitably abbreviated, have been used throughout with the addition of +, and occasionally –, to indicate the full spread of difficulty. Some grades have been changed slightly from those which have become generally accepted over the years. In the main these changes have consisted of down-grading a climb which, with modern equipment, has become better protected than it once was.

Technical grades appear directly on the topos, pinpointing cruxes. The full range of grades, and their approximate international equivalents, are as follows:

British Adjectival Grade		Technical	UIAA	USA
E	Easy		I	
M	Moderate		II	
D	Difficult		III−	
D+	Hard Difficult		III	
VD	Very Difficult		III+	
VD+	Hard Very Difficult		IV−	
S−	Mild Severe		IV	
S	Severe	*4a*	IV	
S+	Hard Severe	4a *4b*	IV+	5.6
VS−	Mild Very Severe	4a *4b* 4c	V	5.6
VS	Very Severe	4b *4c* 5a	V+	5.7
VS+	Very Severe (Hard)	*4c* *5a*	VI−	5.8
HVS	Hard Very Severe	4c *5a* 5b	VI	5.9
E1	Mild Extremely Severe	5a *5b* 5c	VI+/VII−	5.10a/b
E2	Extremely Severe	5b *5c*	VII	5.10c/d

Interpreting Grades: The adjectival, or overall, grade takes into account the seriousness of the route as well as its pure technical difficulty. However, the range of technical difficulties likely to be encountered at a given overall grade is limited. This range is indicated on the table (the most common grade is italicised). Occasionally a + may be added to HVS or E1 grades to indicate a 'top end' route. An unusual combination of adjectival and technical grades reveals a great deal about the route. Consider Communist Convert (VS, 4b) and Central Buttress (HVS, 5b). From these particular combinations we assume, correctly as it happens, that major technical difficulties on Communist Convert will be low in standard but prolonged and serious, whereas those on Central Buttress will be high in standard but short and comparatively safe.

Regional Variations: Lakes technical grades will be found easier than those in outcrop areas but the seriousness of multi-pitch mountain routes to some extent negates this advantage.

WINTER ROUTES

If you are contemplating winter climbing for the first time, please take advice and instruction beforehand on equipment and techniques. Winter climbing is always very serious and front points are no substitute for experience. This guide describes only the routes, not how to climb them, nor how to stay alive in a hostile winter environment.

Snow & Ice Conditions: The Lakes comes a poor third after Scotland and Wales in terms of winter climbing, and many of the harder routes may not come into condition at all in lean years. Proximity to the sea has a lot to do with this and consequently the most reliable ice is to be found in the Helvellyn Range and on Great End – well away from the Gulf Stream. However, large quantities of snow can build up remarkably quickly and avalanches and collapsing cornices cause accidents amongst the unwary almost every year. Be careful out there!

Grading: Winter routes are identified in the contents list by a *W*. They have been graded according to the familiar Scottish system (though being less remote, and by implication less serious, they may seem technically harder, grade for grade).

I   Simple snow gullies, possibly containing a small ice step or cornice. Uncomplicated ridges.
II   Snow gullies with some small pitches. Exposed ridges with rock steps and arêtes.
III   Gullies with long pitches, some of which may be problematical. Escapable or low-angle ice falls.
IV   Major gullies with difficult pitches. Steep ice-falls of continuous difficulty.
V   Major gullies with additional difficulties. Ice-falls which include long vertical sections.

Gradings vary enormously according to conditions and in some cases a borderline grade, such as III/IV, has been allocated. Some grade IV routes which are felt to be hard for their grade but not quite V are given IV/V.

Equipment: It is assumed that twin tools will be used on all but the simplest outings, and that for ice routes these will have steeply inclined picks. Ice screws will be useful on most of the harder routes, and a deadman on the easier ones. A few pegs and a small selection of nuts and slings are normally carried on routes graded III and above.

   Other essential winter equipment includes: helmet, spare food and clothing for enforced bivouacs, headtorch with spare bulb and battery (to enable avoiding same), survival bag, spare mitts, map and compass, and the ability to use them. Remember – 'There is no royal road to safety for the befogged novice on the fells'. Owen Glynne Jones, *Rock Climbing in the English Lake District* (1897).

Timing: Monitor weather and ground conditions and set out very early to get the best from Lakeland winter climbing. A late start is often regretted but an early one seldom is. Your reward will be smaller queues, optimum conditions, fewer benightments, a warm feeling of smugness, and a longer life.

ACCESS

Thankfully the Lakes have long been spared the access problems that plague the rest of the country. In the main this happy state of affairs is due partly to the fact that the National Trust own nearly every crag, and partly to the exemplary behaviour of climbers in past years. Unfortunately a loud-mouthed, litter-dropping, wall-damaging element has been sighted more and more of late – often it is sad to see as part of 'organised' groups.

   Please keep to the footpaths and be courteous to local people at all times. TAKE YOUR LITTER HOME WITH YOU. Do not park so as to block lanes or gateways for large vehicles. Do not let your dog off the lead, however well it heels, anywhere near sheep or on enclosed land. The farmer doesn't know if it's under control and neither do the sheep. If you introduce people to the hills who have not had a rural upbringing, then it is your duty to imbue them with the necessary sense of responsibility – preferably before they arrive. In short, know the country code and abide by it. In this way access will be preserved for yourself and others to enjoy.

METRIC UNITS

I've had to follow the example of previous books in this series in using metric units throughout – for which I apologise sincerely. To get a rough conversion from metres to feet, multiply by three and then add a bit for good measure (a tenth to be more precise). Or, think of them as rather large yards.

MORE INFORMATION

Weather: Recorded forecast available by telephone (Windermere 5151).

Maps: Ordnance Survey maps are useful for locating crags and essential for navigation on the fells. The whole area is covered on the Lake District One Inch *Tourist Map* and also, in greater detail, by the four 1:25,000 *Outdoor Leisure Maps* of The English Lakes.

Comprehensive Guidebooks: The Fell and Rock Climbing Club publish an excellent set of comprehensive guides to Lake District rock climbing. In addition, Cicerone Press publish a guide to winter climbs. These are most useful once regular visits have begun to exhaust the possibilities contained in this book.

Tourist Information: For help with accommodation and so on, ring Windermere 6499 or Keswick 72645.

National Park Information: Further tourist information. Ring Windermere 6601 or Keswick 72803.

Public Transport: British Rail – trains to Windermere, Ulverston, Penrith, Ravenglass and Whitehaven. Ravenglass and Eskdale Railway (Tel: Ravenglass 116). Ribble – many bus services including Windermere–Ambleside–Langdale (Tel: Kendal 33221). Cumberland Motor Services – North-West Lakes including Borrowdale (Tel: Whitehaven 63222). Fell Bus – Buttermere (Tel: Keswick 72403). Mountain Goat – Ambleside, Ullswater, Keswick, Borrowdale and Buttermere (Tel: Windermere 5161).

A FINAL CAUTIONARY NOTE

It has often been remarked that climbing is a lot more pleasurable than writing about it. The authors, who initially had hoped that writing would provide a good excuse for even more climbing, are now in a position to confirm the validity of the above statement. Unfortunately, successive wet summers and winters, though providing plenty of time for writing, have precluded re-checking some routes. It is possible that there will be errors. Hopefully they will not amount to anything more serious than the odd spelling mistake, but if you have problems following any of these climbs you would be wise to trust your own intuition rather than slavishly following the dotted line.

Possible errors by the authors are not the only reason to stay alert; drastic changes can take place on the rock itself, and though it is to be hoped that the majority of routes in this book will be around for some years yet, trees will wither, ledges erode, and holds – or even whole crags – collapse.

If you do experience any difficulty using this guide, whether due to an error on our part or for some other reason, or if you are able to put forenames to initials in the first ascents sections, then please write to Stephen Reid, care of The Crowood Press. We would be very grateful, and your help would be acknowledged in future revisions.

Wasdale

Wasdale, the birthplace of British climbing, retains much of its original charm. This despite one major drawback: the weather which rolls in relentlessly from the Irish Sea. But though the great peaks draw the clouds like magnets there is still no finer place to climb in Lakeland.

Scafell provides the greatest challenges. Its vast and popular North Face gives long routes of all grades on excellent rock. By contrast the East Buttress is often deserted, yet the rock here, a gorgeous ruddy gold hue, is even better, promising perfect friction and positive holds. The same good rock is met on Gable, with the added benefit of sunshine, and the Napes ridges have an alpine feel. For those who tire of long walk-ins, that to Buckbarrow is short, and the climbing sweet.

Few people live in Wasdale; the hillsides are inhospitable and the major part of the valley is occupied by the gigantic brooding presence of Wastwater. But a small settlement thrives at Wasdale Head, much as it must always have done.

Approaches: Wasdale is a cul-de-sac entered from the south-west via the north-western shore of Wastwater. From the south approach via the A595 and Santon Bridge (or take the short cut, snow permitting, from Broughton-in-Furness across Birker Fell). From the north-west approach via Gosforth. From the east, the spectacular Wrynose and Hard Knott Passes are often impassable due to ice in winter and tourists in summer (the latter being by far the most dangerous) and so, although longer, the Birker Fell approach is often quicker.

The nearest railway station is at Seascale (plus a miniature line from Ravenglass to Eskdale Green). There is no bus service, though Mountain Goat run summer tour coaches from Keswick, Ambleside, and Windermere.

The walk over the Styhead Pass takes about 1hr 30mins.

Accommodation: *Camping*: National Trust campsite (with shop) at the head of Wastwater and a smaller site at Wasdale Head.
High camps/bivouacs: Hollowstones under Scafell is traditional though bumpy (spring left of the entrance to the upper coombe). The good flat bivi site under the East Buttress has one drawback; the water supply which often drips from the overhangs above. For Gable there is beautiful high-level camping at Styhead Tarn.
Youth Hostels: Wasdale Hall (GR:145 045).
Hotels: The historic Wasdale Head Inn, plus several guest houses.

Services: The nearest pubs are at Wasdale Head, Strands and Santon Bridge; all serve meals. The Barn Door shop at Wasdale Head sells climbing equipment and some food. Garage at Gosforth and Whitehaven.

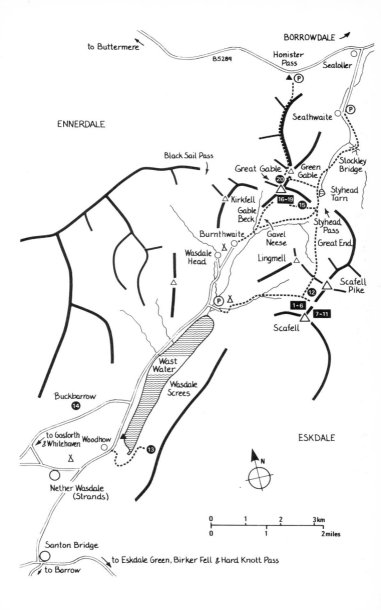

SCAFELL APPROACHES

1   From Wasdale: Park in the National Trust car park at the head of
Wastwater (GR:182 076) and follow a track due east through scrub along
Lingmell Ghyll. Once in open country the ghyll divides and the path
follows what Oppenheimer jokingly called 'a mile more of easy tramping
up a grassy tongue between two chattering brooks.' This is the notorious
Brown Tongue, its sole merit is brevity (and even that is in considerable
doubt). The combe at the top is Hollowstones from where the main cliffs
of Scafell are first revealed. Ahead, the col of Mickledore divides Scafell
from Scafell Pike. The rocks to the left, on the flank of Scafell Pike, are
Pike's Crags. The East Buttress is hidden on the far side of Mickledore.
The crags and gullies of Scafell Crag can be identified from the sketch
opposite. Nearly all its climbs are gained from Rake's Progress, a narrow
path (with some scrambling) that runs under the foot of the cliff. A lower
walker's path runs from Mickledore to Lord's Rake. (GR:208 069). 1hr
30mins.
2   From Eskdale: Approach as for Esk Buttress (see Eskdale area
introduction). Mickledore and the East Buttress will be seen high up to the
left of Esk Buttress and are reached by wearying toil. 2hrs.

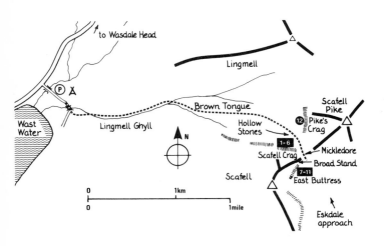

SCAFELL DESCENTS

All descents are serious and can be difficult to find in bad weather. Directions are given looking out.

1 Broad Stand: This scrambly rock climb, graded Difficult, takes the easiest line between the East Buttress and Scafell Crag. Serious in bad or winter conditions, it has been the scene of many accidents. Easy scrambling leads down the left flank (looking out) of Mickledore Chimney. Slightly to the left a polished overhanging corner (not easy to find on first acquaintance but usually marked by cairns) leads to a platform. Down to the left again, a deep cleft leads on to the eastern side of Mickledore. Initially worth reconnoitring from below.
2 Lord's Rake: From the small summit of Symond's Knott, 400m north of the true summit, descend north-west to a narrow rake (difficult to find). This slants down right (looking out) behind the top of the Shamrock to the foot of Deep Ghyll, crossing two cols (poor rock).
3 Deep Ghyll and West Wall Traverse: Descend Deep Ghyll until a traverse leads across its left wall (looking out) on to Lord's Rake (poor rock).
4 Emergency Descent: A safe descent in serious conditions is to descend on a bearing of west-by-south-west to Wastwater. Take care with the cliff-tops until past Symond's Knott.

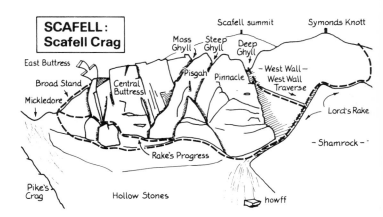

1: (a) Thompson's Route (VD) 50m
(b) Woodhead's Climb (S–) 50m

Summary: Two short routes with an impact out of all proportion to their length. Some doubtful holds.

First Ascent: Thompson's Route – Philip and Peter Thompson, June 1900. Woodhead's Climb – Arthur Woodhead and W.L. Collinson, August 1907 (the second pitch was added by Siegfried Wedgewood Herford and Stanley Jeffcoat, July 1913).

Best Conditions: South-west facing at 800m. Allow four dry days. The rock is slippery when wet.

Approach: Refer to 'Scafell Approaches' at the beginning of this section and to Route 6 diagram. These routes lie on the back of the Pinnacle and are best reached by descending Deep Ghyll after climbing one of the Pinnacle Face Routes (Route 2). Otherwise ascend the West Wall Traverse (*see* Descent 3 of 'Scafell Descents' page 19) to the foot of Professor's Chimney.

Starting Point: Woodhead's starts at the blunt arête formed where the Deep Ghyll face of the Pinnacle meets the left wall of Professor's Chimney. Thompson's begins by climbing Professor's Chimney for a few metres.

Descent: Both routes finish on High Man, from where a short descent (D) leads to the Jordan Gap. The wall ahead is D+ but can be turned on the left. Now refer to 'Scafell Descents'.

It is impossible to date the birth of rock climbing as an independent sport, but the 'Golden Age' of European alpinism undoubtedly induced a reflected interest in our home mountains. Men such as Charles Baumgartner, Cecil Slingsby and Frederick Bowring took in many hard scrambles whilst hill walking, and the Wasdale Hotel, kept by 'Auld Will' Ritson, was a popular sojourn.

A real impetus was provided in the early 1880s by a young Oxford undergraduate, Walter Parry Haskett Smith. Bowring introduced him to the fells and also to John Robinson, a local cragsman who was to become a regular climbing partner. In 1882 Haskett Smith systematically explored the Lakeland crags, making seven new routes on cliffs as far apart as Gimmer and Pillar Rock. Two years later, and despite Ritson's assertion that 'nobbut a fleein' thing'll ever get up theer', he ascended Scafell Pinnacle via the Jordan Gap.

The Pinnacle exerted an impulsive draw on the early climbers and it received the kind of exploration normally reserved for an outcrop. Several of the Face routes are described next, whereas here are the two best from Deep Ghyll. Though short they are remarkably exposed.

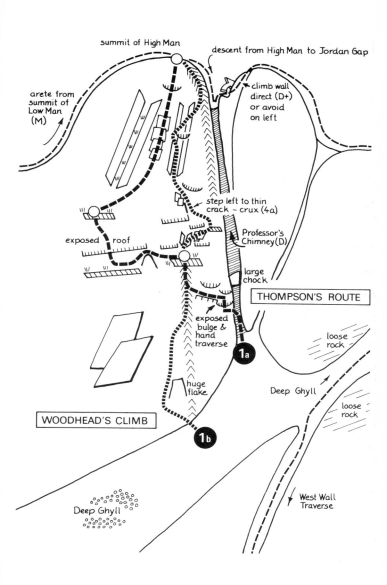

2: PINNACLE FACE ROUTES

   (a) High Man via Steep Ghyll & Slingsby's
       Chimney (VD) 110m
   (b) Hopkinson's Gully (VS–) 100m
   (c) Jones's Route Direct from Lord's Rake (S+) 100m
   (d) Hopkinson's Cairn Direct, Bad Corner
       & Jones's Arête (S)
   (e) Moss Ledge Direct (VS–) 100m

Summary: These routes are not particularly well protected by modern standards. However, the rock is excellent and responds well to the confident yet cautious approach.

First Ascent: Slingsby's Chimney – William Cecil Slingsby, Geoffrey Hastings, Edward Hopkinson and Walter Parry Haskett Smith, July 1888. Jones's Arête – Owen Glynne Jones, Ashley and George Abraham, April 1896. Jones's Route – Jones and G.T. Walker, April 1898. Hopkinson's Cairn Direct – Siegfried Herford and George Sansom, April 1912. Hopkinson's Gully – Herford and Sansom, June 1912. Bad Corner – Harry Kelly, George Bower, Emily Kelly and R.E.W Pritchard, June 1919. Moss Ledge

Direct – Fergus Graham and G.M. Wellburn, September 1925.

Best Conditions: North facing at 800m. Allow four dry days. The rock is very slippery when wet.

Approach: Refer to 'Scafell Approaches' page 18 and Route 6. The Pinnacle is reached by a 50m scramble, starting from just left of Deep Ghyll. Alternatively, start up Steep Ghyll and take to grass on the right (easier).

Starting Point: Refer to diagram.

Descent: From the summit of Low Man, a knife edge arête (M) leads to the summit of High Man. Descend as for Route 1.

Following Haskett Smith's ascent of High Man, the Hopkinson brothers descended the Pinnacle Face as far as a large ledge where Edward built a cairn. That same winter, in an attempt to reach the cairn from Lord's Rake, Charles Hopkinson led a party some considerable distance up the gully which now bears his name before ice forced a retreat. Jones's epic ascent of his route in stockinged feet solved the problem of a direct climb up the face, but the lure of Hopkinson's Cairn remained. Many failed attempts culminated in 1903 when four climbers were killed.

   The spell was broken in 1912 when Sansom resumed exploration by descending on a top rope from the Crevasse. Before the year was out, Herford and he had repeated Jones's Route, reached Hopkinson's Cairn from Lord's Rake, and completed the ascent of Hopkinson's Gully.

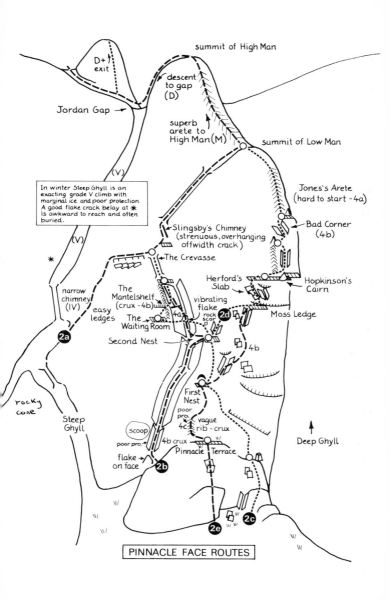

summit of High Man

D+ exit

Jordan Gap →

descent to gap (D)

superb arete to High Man (M)

summit of Low Man

Jones's Arete (hard to start - 4a)

Bad Corner (4b)

(V)

In winter Steep Ghyll is an exacting grade V climb with marginal ice and poor protection. A good flake crack belay at ✳ is awkward to reach and often buried.

Slingsby's Chimney (strenuous, overhanging offwidth crack)

The Crevasse

Herford's Slab

Hopkinson's Cairn

(V)

✳

The Mantelshelf (crux - 4b)

vibrating flake

rock scar

Moss Ledge

2d

narrow chimney (IV)

easy ledges

The Waiting Room

4a

Second Nest

2a

4b

First Nest

poor pro.

vague rib - crux

4c

rocky cone

Deep Ghyll

Steep Ghyll

scoop

poor pro.

4b crux

Pinnacle Terrace

flake on face

2b

2e

2c

PINNACLE FACE ROUTES

3: MOSS GHYLL (S or III/IV) 130m

Summary: A marvellous gully climb, steeped in history. Many of the difficulties can be turned, though the best of them are unavoidable. Highly recommended in winter. Helmets are advisable at all times. (Illustrated on Route 4 diagram)

First Ascent: Prof. J. Norman Collie, Geoffrey Hastings and John Wilson Robinson, December 1892 (Collier's Chimney was climbed the following day by a party led by Dr. Joseph Collier; Owen Glynne Jones climbed Moss Ghyll in true winter conditions in 1893).

Best Conditions: North facing at 800m. Any conditions will suffice, but at its best in winter. Can hold good ice quite late in the season.

Approach: Refer to 'Scafell Approaches' at the beginning of this section and to Route 6 diagram.

Starting Point: Traverse left along Rake's Progress from Steep Ghyll. Moss Ghyll is the next gully on the left. The first pitches can be avoided on the right (D).

Descent: Refer to 'Scafell Descents' at the beginning of this section.

The earliest mountaineering routes were the 'easy ways', the Old West and Jack's Rake for example. The next obvious points of attack were the gullies and chimneys. Moss Ghyll, one of the most compelling of these lines, withstood some determined assaults. Even Haskett Smith was turned back by smooth walls at the enormous chockstone.

The party that eventually triumphed had the advantage of having reconnoitred the amphitheatre from above, but they met with the same problems at the chockstone as their predecessors. Collie's first attempt at the traverse ended when he slipped from the tiny holds and was skilfully fielded by Hastings. On his second try he succeeded, but only by using a freshly hacked foothold – the infamous 'Collie Step'. He thereby set a startling precedent which unfortunately appears to undergo periodic revivals. Afterwards he recorded that Hastings's axe was none the worse for the experiment. Oh that the ethics of British climbing had been as resilient!

'The situation was almost critical, but not an unusual one for winter climbing in Cumberland.' – Owen Glynne Jones, *Rock Climbing in the English Lake District* (1897).

The Collie Step, Moss Ghyll (Route 3).
  (Climber: Walter Phipps. Photo: Stephen Reid.)

4: (a) Moss Ghyll Grooves (S+) 90m
(b) Slab and Groove Route (VS+) 80m

Summary: Excellent, steep slab climbing on the best rock face in the Lakes. Good protection in most places.

First Ascent: Moss Ghyll Grooves – Harry Mills Kelly, Blanche Eden-Smith and J.B Kilshaw, July 1926. Slab and Groove Route – Jim Birkett and Len Muscroft, August 1948.

Best Conditions: North facing at 800m. Allow four dry summer days.

Approach: Both routes start in Moss Ghyll. Refer to Route 3.

Starting Point: Climb up to the right flank of Moss Ghyll until the Gully can be regained where it widens above a steep chimney. A vague slanting groove runs up to the left and marks the start of Moss Ghyll Grooves. Slab and Groove begins higher up Moss Ghyll at a big slab capped by an overhang opposite Tennis Court Wall.

Descent: Refer to 'Scafell Descents' at the beginning of this section.

It is surprising that the team that would triumph on Central Buttress should fail on Moss Ghyll Grooves, but so it was. The route was left to Kelly, who finally succeeded after seven years of consideration, inspections and cleaning expeditions – a typically careful approach. Being a firm believer in the equality of women, he would have had no qualms in inviting so bold a climber as Mrs Eden-Smith to be his second. Indeed, he recorded that she took a precarious, belay-less stance some way up the second pitch purely so she could encourage him on the crux. This involves what she described as 'a stride on to a small protuberance about the size of a damson stone' in order to make a thin traverse out on to the arête of an extremely airy slab. The exposure thereafter is pitiless, almost to the final moves, and the situations attained seem outrageous for Hard Severe.

However, Kelly's contribution to Lakeland climbing was far greater than just the sum of his new routes, splendid though they are. With his scientific advocation of 'rubbers' over 'nails', his use of top-roped inspection, down-climbing and sophisticated ropework, and his brilliant editorship of the Fell and Rock climbing guides, he introduced a new and refreshing approach to the climbing scene in the aftermath of the First World War. Greater numbers were able to climb in the hills as a result, and greater numbers climbed hard.

Slab and Groove was Jim Birkett's final addition to these great cliffs and, though much shorter, makes a fine companion.

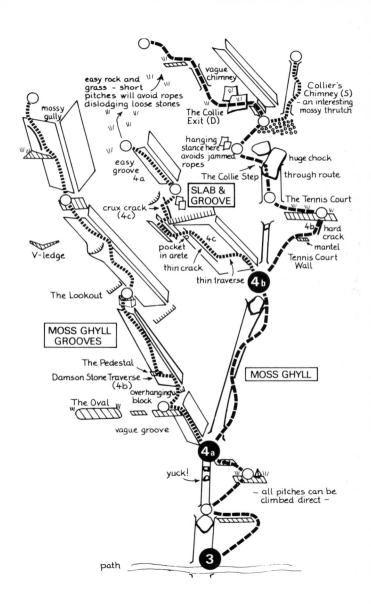

Jones's Route (Route 2c).
   (Photo: Steve Ashton.)

The Great Flake, Central Buttress (Route 5).
  (Photo: Steve Ashton.)

5: CENTRAL BUTTRESS (HVS) 140m

Summary: A grand route that represented a massive leap forward in the standards of difficulty of its day. The crux flake offers the modern protagonist exactly the same protection as it did the first ascentionists: its few short feet contrive to make a demanding lead.

First Ascent: Siegfried Herford, George Sansom and Claude Holland, April 1914 (over two days and using combined tactics on the Great Flake). First climbed free by Menlove Edwards, William Stallybrass and Marco Pallis, August 1931. Direct Finish added by F. Graham Balcombe, Jerry Wright and J. Robert Files, June 1934.

Direct Start added by A. Mullan and Harry Thompson, July 1939.

Best Conditions: North facing at 800m and slow to dry. Allow four dry summer days.

Approach: Refer to 'Scafell Approaches' page 18, and Route 6 diagram. Traverse left along Rake's Progress, passing Moss Ghyll.

Starting Point: At a narrow leftward-slanting ramp some 10m left of Moss Ghyll. This is just before Rake's Progress rises up a short wide chimney.

Descent: Refer to 'Scafell Descents', page 19.

It is hard now to imagine the effect of the First World War on the Lakeland climbing scene of 1914. Not only did it bring a virtual halt to all activity for four years, but it cruelly robbed the hills of some of their greatest explorers. One of the finest of these was Siegfried Wedgewood Herford, who was killed in action in France in 1916. Gritstone trained, his influence on Scafell was short but immense. Central Buttress, the culmination of his efforts and deservedly one of the most famous climbs in Britain, is his epitaph.

Herford had spent some time examining the face and, with Stanley Jeffcoat, had inspected the Flake from above. He actually managed to climb it unaided on a top rope, but subsequently failed to lead it. In the end Sansom tied himself to the chockstone while Herford, who had removed his boots, swarmed over him to reach good holds, uttering as he did so the heartfelt remark: 'I'm glad our mothers can't see us in this place!'

Modern climbers, following Edwards's 1931 example, will secure only the rope to that most famous of English chockstones before committing themselves to a series of arm-draining laybacks to the best-loved jug on the crag. Nothing else on this climb is as difficult, though the delicate rightward traverse to the V-ledge adds to one's awe of Herford's magnificent achievement.

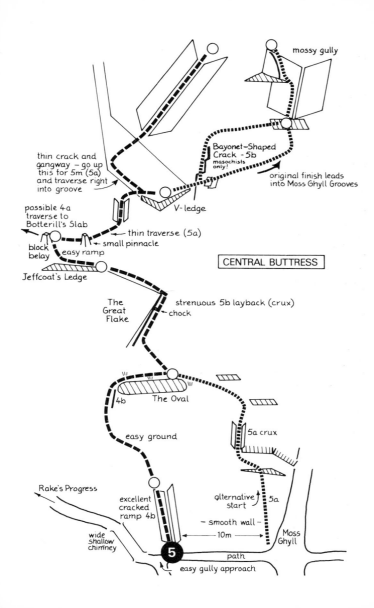

mossy gully

thin crack and
gangway – go up
this for 5m (5a)
and traverse right
into groove

Bayonet-Shaped
Crack – 5b
masochists
only!

original finish leads
into Moss Ghyll Grooves

possible 4a
traverse to
Botterill's Slab

V-ledge

thin traverse (5a)

block
belay   easy ramp

small pinnacle

CENTRAL BUTTRESS

Jeffcoat's Ledge

The
Great
Flake

strenuous 5b layback (crux)

chock

The Oval

4b

easy ground

5a crux

excellent
cracked
ramp 4b

alternative
start

5a

Rake's Progress

wide
shallow
chimney

– smooth wall –

10m

Moss
Ghyll

5

path

easy gully approach

6: BOTTERILL'S SLAB (VS) 100m

Summary: Sustained slab climbing on small holds (especially by the harder option). Fine rock and a splendid setting. Exposed.

First Ascent: Fred Botterill, H Williamson and J.E. Grant, June 1903.

Best Conditions: North facing at 800m. Allow four dry days.

Approach: Refer to 'Scafell Approaches' page 18. Traverse left along Rake's Progress, passing Moss Ghyll and Central Buttress, until under the huge, pale, left-slanting slab.

Starting Point: At a short chimney in line with the slab.

Descent: Refer to 'Scafell Descents' page 19.

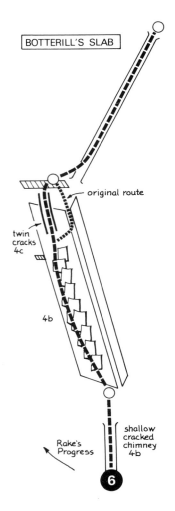

BOTTERILL'S SLAB

original route

twin cracks 4c

4b

Rake's Progress

shallow cracked chimney 4b

6

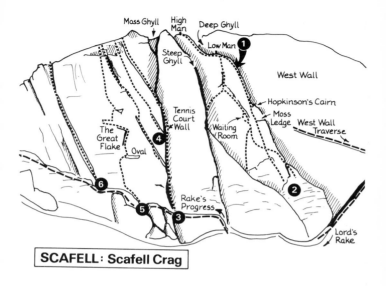

SCAFELL: Scafell Crag

Fred Botterill's ascent of his slab was a remarkable affair. Not only was it a grade harder than anything climbed previously, but it involved an exposed and totally unprotected hundred foot run-out. He wore nailed boots, clutched an ice axe – at times in his teeth – and towed up eighty feet of heavy rope. Think of that as you insert yet another RP in the crux and chalk up your fingers.

Using the ice axe to clean moss from miniscule holds, Botterill made cautious progress up the left edge of the slab until hard moves brought him to a welcome, but tiny, ledge. It was whilst removing grass one-handed from this that it providentially dropped the axe which stuck quivering in Rake's Progress. While sitting on the ledge he spied a lady far below and, recalling a book of etiquette which claimed that 'a gentleman in whatever situation of life should never forget his manners towards the other sex', calmly raised his hat. A further sixty feet of hemp were tied on to enable him to reach the relative safety of the crack on the right.

Botterill's ascent, a few months before the Pinnacle tragedy, marked the end of a golden age. Though of outstanding ability, he was not by nature ambitious. He went on to make other climbs, but few of them came even close to approaching the Slab in either difficulty or daring and, after 1909 when his partner died in an accident on the Napes, he never climbed seriously again.

7: MICKLEDORE GROOVES (VS) 80m

Summary: A true classic. Sustained with good protection and outstanding situations. When dry the Direct Finish provides a worthwhile continuation at the same grade.

First Ascent: Colin Kirkus, Ivan Waller and Marco Pallis, May 1931 (the Direct Finish was added by Dennis English, David Beattie and Michael McKenzie, May 1959).

Best Conditions: East facing at 800m. Allow two dry summer days.

Approach: Refer to 'Scafell Approaches' page 18. From Mickledore,

the col between Scafell Pike and Scafell, go round to the left (looking in), passing the narrow cleft of Broad Stand until below the large gully of Mickledore Chimney.

Starting Point: Start about 20m left of Mickledore Chimney and about 10m right of a well-made bivi site. Refer to Route 9 diagram. A short steep wall gives access to a right-slanting ramp which leads to twin grooves.

Descent: Refer to 'Scafell Descents' page 19. Alternatively, descend steep grass well to the left of Hell's Groove (Route 11).

Colin Kirkus, famed for his bold climbing on delicate slabs and a steady stream of magnificent new routes on Cloggy, Dinas Mot and at Ogwen, was rather an outsider to the Lakeland climbing scene, so it must have rankled somewhat with the Fell and Rock luminaries when he made the first ascent of the highly impressive East Buttress of Scafell.

The occasion was a Wayfarers' meet and the Lakes were blessed with sunshine. Kirkus together with Ivan Waller, Marco Pallis and Richard Nicholson, walked from Langdale to Mickledore, pausing for a swim in Angle Tarn. Kirkus, climbing in gym shoes, led the route in three pitches with a characteristic minimum of fuss. The final 45m were climbed in one run out, with no protection, and took him just three-quarters of an hour. Nicholson photographed events from an advantageous viewpoint whilst Waller and Pallis seconded. Kirkus and Waller then climbed Moss Ghyll Grooves before the party made their leisurely way back over the tops to Langdale – a good day by any standards.

The route is the among the finest on the crag, with excellent climbing throughout on the beautifully clean rock typical of the East Buttress.

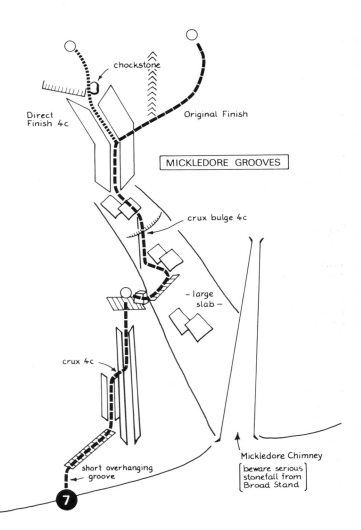

chockstone

Direct
Finish 4c

Original Finish

MICKLEDORE GROOVES

crux bulge 4c

– large
slab –

crux 4c

short overhanging
groove

7

Mickledore Chimney
[beware serious
stonefall from
Broad Stand]

8: THE CENTAUR (HVS+) 110m

Summary: A long and sustained climb at the upper limit of its grade. Clever route finding combined with the superb rock of the East Buttress make it one of the most memorable outings on the crag.

First Ascent: Les Brown and Steve Read, June 1960.

Best Conditions: East facing at 800m. Allow three dry days.

Approach: Refer to 'Scafell Approaches' page 18. From Mickledore, the col between Scafell Pike and Scafell, go round to the left (looking in), passing under the large gully of Mickledore Chimney until 5m left of the lowest point of the East Buttress. (Refer also to Route 9 diagram.)

Starting Point: Easy rocks lead to a ledge at 3m (the broken leftward-slanting ramp line starting from the left of the ledge is Great Eastern – Route 9). Centaur starts up a short, left-leaning groove at the right end of this ledge.

Descent: Refer to 'Scafell Descents' page 19. Alternatively, descend steep grass well to the left of Hell's Groove (Route 11).

For those of romantic bent the name 'Centaur' might conjour up a fleeting vision: of the freedom of thundering hooves, of distant mythical times and lands, of death before dishonour. Noble notions in our humdrum age.

But let's put aside such rubbish and get down to the rock. One expects the best where Les Brown is concerned, and that's exactly what you get. His routes may be few but they are all excellent and during his active period in the early 1960s he acquired an enviable reputation for quietly picking off plums. The list is impressive – Gormenghast, Nazgul, Sidewalk and Praying Mantis, to name just a handful. He worked in secret, startling competitors by producing aces out of the blue. Praying Mantis, for instance, was gardened over winter, leaving the lowest reaches till last. On another occasion he trailed a red herring by dropping hints to rivals that he was engaged in exploring the imaginary Far East Buzzard Crag.

Centaur takes such an obvious line that it had been the target of several previous attempts. But it took Brown to realise that the best way of climbing the groove was in fact not to climb the groove at all and to work out a route up the steep wall above the Great Eastern traverse. And just where a lesser climb might turn to scrambling, Centaur unveils a brilliant finale in the shape of a perpendicular thirty foot layback crack. A noble end indeed.

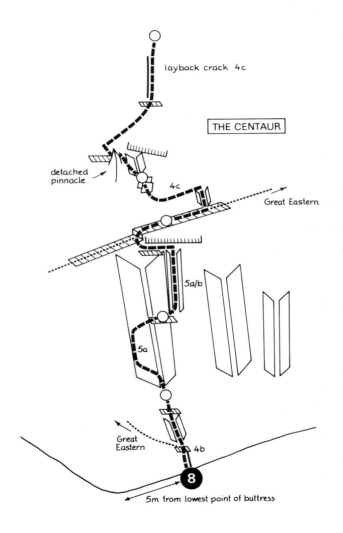

layback crack 4c

THE CENTAUR

detached
pinnacle

4c

Great Eastern

5a/b

5a

Great
Eastern

4b

8

5m from lowest point of buttress

9: (a) Great Eastern Route (VS) 80m
(b) Yellow Slab (HVS) 80m

Summary: A pair of marvellously exposed routes, low in technical difficulty but serious because of the quantity of traversing involved. A fall might well place the climber in a difficult position and prusik loops should be carried.

First Ascent: Great Eastern Route – Maurice Linnell and Sid Cross, August 1932. Yellow Slab – Maurice Linnell and H. Pearson, September 1933.

Best Conditions: East facing at 800m. Allow two dry summer days after bad weather for Great Eastern. The jamming crack on Yellow Slab can take much longer to dry.

Approach: Refer to 'Scafell Approaches' page 18. From Mickledore, the col between Scafell Pike and Scafell, go round to the left (looking in), passing under the large gully of Mickledore Chimney, until 5m left of the lowest point of the East Buttress.

Starting Point: Easy rocks lead to a ledge at 3m. The broken, leftward-slanting ramp line from the left end of the ledge is common to both routes.

Descent: Refer to 'Scafell Descents' page 19. Alternatively, descend steep grass well to the left of Hell's Groove (Route 11).

Be warned at the outset that, despite low technical grades, these two interlopers in the extreme territory of the East Buttress are not for the faint-hearted. A steady head will be required throughout, not least on the part of the leader in the selfless arrangement of protection. Unextended runners on such complex rising traverses are likely to be lifted out as the rope is taken in, leaving the poor second to contemplate the possibility of an awesome swing. This is unlikely to improve anyone's climbing ability.

Both routes were the work of Maurice Linnell, a very daring climber who was to die in an avalanche on Ben Nevis the year following his Yellow Slab ascent. The unfulfilled promise of this outstanding young man can only be glimpsed in the few incredible climbs he put up in a tragically short career. The boldest by far was his solo ascent in 1932 of the Bayonet-Shaped Crack finish to Central Buttress (a pitch graded at 5b today, when it is undoubtedly cleaner). But the Yellow Slab and Great Eastern Route are definitely his grandest, and for the competent provide fantastically airy ways up this exciting cliff.

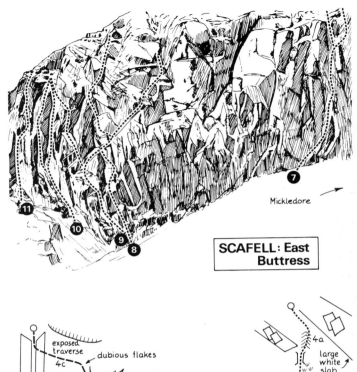

Mickledore

SCAFELL: East Buttress

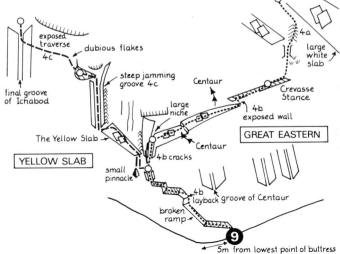

final groove
of Ichabod

exposed
traverse
4c

dubious flakes

steep jamming
groove 4c

Centaur

large
niche

4a

large
white
slab

Crevasse
Stance

The Yellow Slab

4b
exposed wall

Centaur

GREAT EASTERN

YELLOW SLAB

4b cracks

small
pinnacle

4b
layback groove of Centaur

broken
ramp

9

5m from lowest point of buttress

10: (a) Ichabod (E2) 50m
(b) Phoenix (E1) 50m

Summary: Strenuous climbing. Protection is adequate on the many hard moves, with the exception of the second pitch of Phoenix.

First Ascent: Ichabod – Geoff Oliver, Geoff Arkless and Len Willis, May 1960 (2 points aid). Phoenix – Ron Moseley, June 1957 (with one point of aid; the Direct Finish was added by Geoff Cram and Bill Young in June 1967).

Best Conditions: East facing at 800m. Allow three dry days.

Approach: Refer to 'Scafell Approaches' page 18. From Mickledore,

the col between Scafell and Scafell Pike, go round to the left (looking in) to the lowest point of the East Buttress.

Starting Point: 25m to the left of the toe of the buttress, a smooth, easy-angled ramp line (S) slants up left to a little niche below a line of steep corners defining the right-hand side of a towering pillar. Both climbs start from this niche. (Refer also to Route 9 diagram.)

Descent: Refer to 'Scafell Descents' page 19. Alternatively, descend steep grass well to the left of Hell's Groove (Route 11).

'And she named the child Ichabod, saying "The glory is departed. . ."' (I Sam. iv 21).

'. . .the future is bright with the possibility of great developments, a time when there is no danger of the call of Ichabod, a time when we may well feel that the best is yet to come.' (C.F.Holland, F & RCC *Guide to Scafell*, 1936).

Ichabod is a line of such grandeur that the first ascensionists might be forgiven for feeling that the best had now been achieved. The climbing is hard from the start. Tension and an aid peg were used on the delicate traverse across the steep slab, but nowadays the only tension should be in the air as, equipped with all the modern advantages of chalk and 'stickies', you work out the sequence of fingernail moves required to reach poor haven in a shallow corner. The rest of the pitch is just as fingery, but nothing else is as tricky until the final hard balance moves out left lead to easier ground.

    Phoenix arose from the ashes of an earlier attempt on Ichabod and was in its day the hardest climb on the cliff. Reminiscent of Vember, it claims more than its fair share of skin to be 100% enjoyable, but is still fine company for its elegant neighbour.

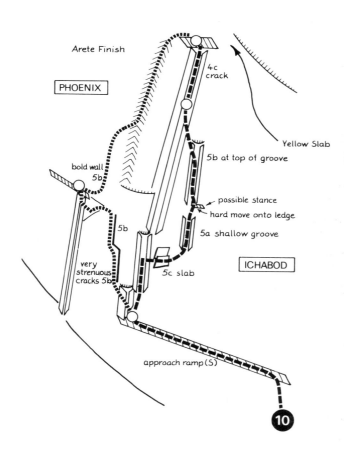

Arete Finish

PHOENIX

4c crack

Yellow Slab

5b at top of groove

bold wall 5b

possible stance

hard move onto ledge

5a shallow groove

5b

ICHABOD

very strenuous cracks 5b

5c slab

approach ramp (S)

10

11: HELL'S GROOVE (HVS+) 80m

Summary: An historically important route offering a series of steep and contrasting pitches at a reasonable standard. If the final pitch is wet the original and much easier finish can be taken.

First Ascent: Pete Greenwood and Arthur Dolphin, May 1952 (Direct Finish added by John Adams and Colin Read, August 1972).

Best Conditions: East facing at 800m. Slower to dry than the other East Buttress climbs. Allow four dry days.

Approach: Refer to 'Scafell Approaches' page 18. From Mickledore, the col between Scafell and Scafell Pike, go round to the left (looking in) to the lowest point of the East Buttress. Descend slightly, follow a path to the left for 10m, and then ascend over mossy ledges towards the foot of a prominent groove to the left of Ichabod. (Refer also to Route 9 diagram.)

Starting Point: The groove is guarded by a 7m wall split by a steep jamming crack – the first pitch. Scramble up from the right to a slab at the foot of the crack.

Descent: Refer to 'Scafell Descents' page 19. Alternatively, descend steep grass well to the left of the crag.

This is probably one of the least climbed three-star HVSs in the Lakes. One can only suppose that folk are put off by the thought of an overhanging jamming crack followed by an overhanging manky groove followed by yet another overhanging jamming crack (the description of this last as 'lurid green' in the present F&RCC guide does little to help). So surprise yourself: find a Gritstone Gorilla to thug up the first twenty feet and then take the lead for the wall to the right of the manky groove and delight (or despair) in the ensuing fly-on-the-wall situations. And if you are tempted to grizzle about the laughable protection – think on this – Dolphin had one hand-inserted piton on the entire pitch.

Now, the next bit is short and will not be nearly ferocious enough to satisfy GG's masochistic tendencies. So point out the enticing possibilities of further blood, sweat and tears on the final crack, where the difficulties are more due to the awkwardness of arranging protection than the actual climbing. You can follow on peacefully, over one of the oddest finishes on the mountain.

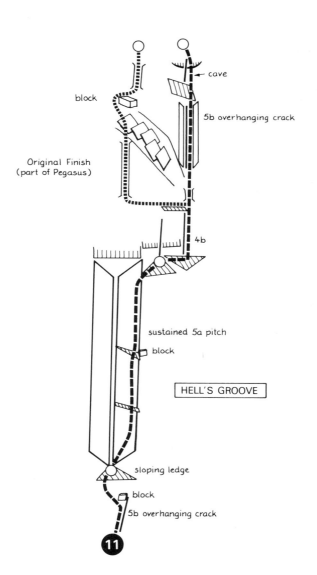

cave

block

5b overhanging crack

Original Finish
(part of Pegasus)

4b

sustained 5a pitch

block

HELL'S GROOVE

sloping ledge

block

5b overhanging crack

11

12: (a) Grooved Arête (VD) 135m
(b) Juniper Buttress (S−) 80m
(c) Wall and Crack Climb (VD+) 90m

Summary: Short pitches and a multiplicity of interesting problems give these routes a traditional flavour.

First Ascent: Grooved Arête − Claude Holland and Gustave Robert Speaker, April 1924 (top pitch added by G. Barrat and T.A.H. Medleycot, March 1934). Juniper Buttress − Harry Kelly, R.E.W. Pritchard, Nigel and Walter Eden-Smith, April 1924. Wall and Crack Climb − Kelly, Pritchard, Blanche Eden-Smith and Graham Wilson, April 1924.

Best Conditions: West facing at 900m. Dries quickly but is greasy when wet. Allow two dry summer days.

Approach: Refer to 'Scafell Approaches' page 18. Pike's Crag stands opposite Scafell's main cliff, on the northern side of Hollowstones. All these climbs lie on Pulpit Rock, which is the central mass of the crag.

Starting Point: Grooved Arête starts under a large overhang just to the right of the long arête which descends from the summit of the crag. Wall and Crack Climb begins at the arête on the left edge of the crag, and Juniper Buttress about 35m to the right at a large block.

Descent: Scramble to the summit and descend a short wall (D) to the gap between the crag and Scafell Pike. Descend the scree gully on the right of the crag, keeping to the left (looking out) of a large pinnacle which splits the gully at its widest point.

There is little glory to be won on Pike's, and no one is likely to become the toast of the Wasdale Head for having made a clean ascent of Wall and Crack Climb or one of its neighbours. As the pitches flow by, each a total contrast. and seemingly detached from its predecessor, it becomes apparent why this huge crag was left virtually undeveloped until the mid-twenties: the staggering view of the vast North Face of Scafell, even through the haze of a warm afternoon, can hardly be avoided at every stance and anyone climbing on Pike's has to suppress a constant niggle in the back of the mind that they are missing out on something better. Well in a way they are. . . but then the rock here is excellent, the crowds, nil; and the climbing, not bad at all. Oh, and one further small blessing: sunshine, all afternoon.

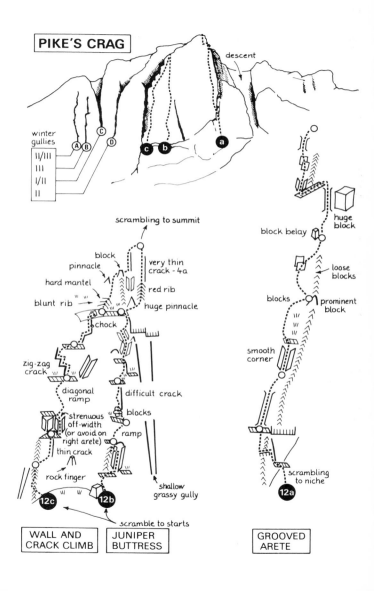

PIKE'S CRAG

descent

winter gullies

A	B	II/III
C		III
D		I/II
		II

c   b   a

scrambling to summit

block
pinnacle

very thin
crack - 4a

hard mantel

red rib

blunt rib

huge pinnacle

chock

zig-zag
crack

difficult crack

diagonal
ramp

strenuous
off-width
(or avoid on
right arete)

blocks

ramp

thin crack

rock finger

shallow
grassy gully

12c   12b

scramble to starts

WALL AND
CRACK CLIMB

JUNIPER
BUTTRESS

huge
block

block belay

loose
blocks

blocks

prominent
block

smooth
corner

scrambling
to niche

12a

GROOVED
ARETE

13: (a) Great Gully (III) 250m
(b) The Right-Hand Finish (IV/V) 100m

Summary: Tremendous traditional gully climbing involving short hard pitches interspersed with large stances. By contrast the Right-Hand Finish is very sustained and lacks good belays.

First Ascent: Norman Collie, Geoffrey Hastings and John Wilson Robinson, winter 1891. Right-Hand Finish — unknown.

Best Conditions: West facing at 300m. Low altitude means that a prolonged cold spell is required. When formed, the Right-Hand Finish shows up well from the road on the far side of Wastwater.

Approach: From the Santon Bridge to Wasdale road. Just before the southern end of Wastwater is a farm called Woodhow (GR:140 042). Parking hereabouts is very limited, but slightly more is available a little further north near Wasdale Hall Youth Hostel. From opposite the farm a footpath leads round the foot of the lake, passing some Water Board buildings.

Starting Point: Follow the path under several lesser gullies, including C Gully, until directly under Great Gully. A short, sharp ascent on semi-scree gains its mouth.

Descent: Climb up to join a vague path along the top of the crags, then make a wide detour to the south.

Lakeland winter climbing is a hit and miss affair and it can be a frustrating experience trying to get days off to coincide with fleeting good conditions. However, when you finally get it right, the experience is all the more rewarding. Who would imagine, for instance, that an ice climb of this magnitude could be so easily accessible? You don't get that on the Ben.

The first few pitches are common to both routes: short ice columns with intimidating bulges, formed by the freezing of cascading waters, mid-tumble from pool to pool. At the Amphitheatre the original route continues in much the same vein. But hidden up right by a short, usually rocky, scramble is the Right-Hand Finish, a great hanging mass of ice fit to rival Hadrian's Wall. The line varies from year to year, but it is generally necessary to teeter leftwards under overhangs before climbing very steeply to an awkward heathery stance. From here the only brave way out is to traverse boldly back into the centre of the icefall, shattering nerves and icicles. Time and distance disappear in this vertical white-out — a stretching rope is your only guide to a poor belay. Another long pitch, encroaching dusk, a summit gale, break the spell.

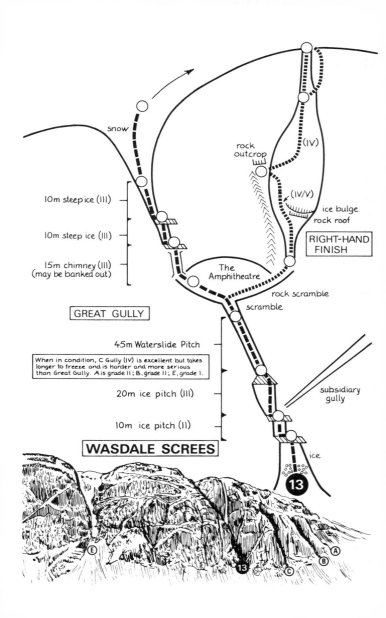

snow

10m steep ice (III)

10m steep ice (III)

15m chimney (III)
(may be banked out)

rock outcrop

(IV)

(IV/V)

ice bulge
rock roof

RIGHT-HAND
FINISH

The
Amphitheatre

rock scramble

scramble

GREAT GULLY

45m Waterslide Pitch

When in condition, C Gully (IV) is excellent but takes
longer to freeze and is harder and more serious
than Great Gully. A is grade II; B, grade II; E, grade I.

20m ice pitch (III)

10m ice pitch (II)

WASDALE SCREES

subsidiary
gully

ice

13

E

13

A
B

C

14: BUCKBARROW CLASSICS

    (a) Gargarin (VD) 65m
    (b) The Mysteron (HVS) 50m
    (c) Imagine (E1) 50m (d) Witch (VS) 45m
    (e) Too Many Hands (E2) 40m
    (f) Buckbarrow Needle (VS) 25m
    (g) Needle Front (E1) 25m
    (h) Needless Eliminate (HVS) 25m

Summary: Extremely good short routes on excellent rock.

First Ascent: Witch – Pat Walsh and Mick Burke, March 1961. Needle Front – John Earl and Paul Stewart, June 1979. Needless Eliminate – Stewart and Earl, June 1979. Imagine – Tony Stephenson and Joe Wilson, April 1981. Too Many Hands – Stephenson, Colin Sice, Wilson and Bill Young, May 1981. Remainder – uncertain.

Best Conditions: South facing at 300m. Often avoids the bad weather of higher crags. All these routes are extremely quick drying except for Too Many Hands, which requires one dry day.

Approach: The Wastwater to Gosforth road runs under the crags which will be seen to the north one mile after leaving the shore of Wastwater. Witch Buttress is the third buttress along from the left (it has a prominent central groove) and can be approached directly from below. GR:135 058. 20 mins. Pike Crag is situated above and just right of Witch Buttress.

Starting Point: Gargarin – at the lowest left-hand edge of Witch Buttress, just right of a gully. Mysteron and Imagine – from the left-hand of two huge detached flakes to the left of the Pinnacle. Witch – at the right-hand side of the Pinnacle. Too Many Hands – 2m right of Witch, under a large wedged block. Buckbarrow Needle – at either the left or right-hand crack of the Needle. Needle Front – at the left-hand crack of Buckbarrow Needle. Needless Eliminate – on stepped ledges just up and right from Buckbarrow Needle.

Descent: Witch Buttress – via a grassy ramp to the right. Pike Crag – walk off left.

Buckbarrow is well sited, facing south on a gentle hillside with a fine view of the Isle of Man set in a shimmering Irish Sea. Across the valley, Wastwater and the Screes brood in gloomy silence – a perfect contrast.

    A keen party of good ability will find this selection makes for an outstanding day, whilst those more intent on scenery and sunbathing can do as little as they wish.

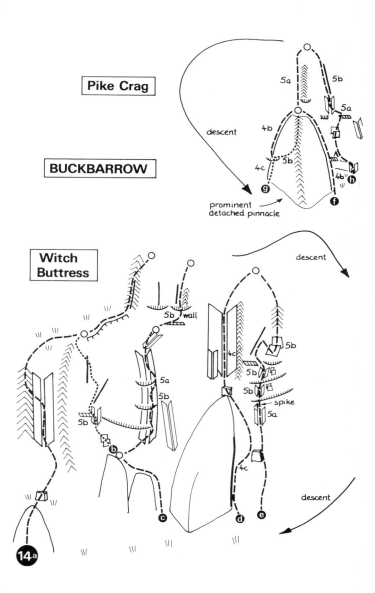

Pike Crag

BUCKBARROW

Witch Buttress

5a   5b
5a
descent
4b
4c   5b
g
prominent
detached pinnacle
f
4b
h

descent

5b   wall
4c   5b
5a   5b   5b
5b   5b
5a
spike
5a
b
c   d   e
4c

descent

14a

15: (a) Kern Knotts Crack (VS −) 20m
(b) Innominate Crack (VS −) 20m
(c) Buttonhook Route (HVS+) 35m

Summary: Three short but technical routes on one of the most pleasantly situated crags in the Lake District. Each is a milestone in the history of rock climbing.

First Ascent: Kern Knotts Crack – Owen Glynne Jones and Hubert Bowen, April 1897. Innominate Crack – George Bower, Bentley Beetham and Jack Wilton, April 1921. Buttonhook Route – Frederick Graham Balcombe and C.J. Astley Cooper, June 1934.

Best Conditions: South facing at 550m. All these climbs are very quick to dry and are situated in a natural sun-trap.

Approach: (1) From Wasdale Head, follow the track to the highest point of Styhead Pass. Turn left (west) at the Mountain Rescue box on to the Gable Traverse path (ill-defined at first) and Kern Knotts will be reached in 3 minutes GR:216 094. 45 mins. (2) From Seathwaite Farm, Borrowdale, a track leads to a small hump-backed bridge (troll in situ). Fork right to Styhead Pass and join approach 1; 1 hr.

Starting Point: The main feature of Kern Knotts, as seen from the approach, is a smooth wall split by an off-width crack on the left and a thinner crack on the right. These are Kern Knotts Crack and Innominate Crack respectively. Button Hook Route takes the prow – start at a steep slab under some overhangs.

Descent: Either by abseil or by descending Kern Knotts Chimney (D) – see diagram. Alternatively climb a continuation slab and make a long detour to left or right.

Owen Glynne Jones, or, as he would have it, the Only Genuine Jones, was very much a modern rock star out of his time. Immensely strong, he was the acknowledged champion of the Billiard Table Traverse and other unusual gymnastic exercises indulged in by the rowdier guests at the Wasdale Head Inn.

Inspired by a photograph of Napes Needle, he began climbing with John Robinson who introduced him to Kern Knotts. The line of the Crack was impelling but Robinson would not hear of it, saying, 'Well Jones, if you climb that crack I'll never speak to you again!' The eventual ascent, involving rather dangerous sounding combined tactics with an ice-axe, attracted some criticism. However, like the later Innominate Crack and Buttonhook Route, it was technically among the hardest climbs of the day. Protection on all these routes was, of course, virtually nil. One suspects that their leaders were a breed apart.

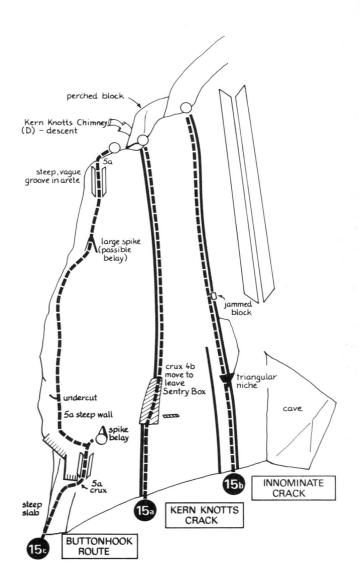

perched block

Kern Knotts Chimney
(D) – descent

steep, vague
groove in arête

5a

large spike
(possible
belay)

jammed
block

crux 4b
move to
leave
Sentry Box

triangular
niche

undercut

5a steep wall

cave

spike
belay

5a
crux

steep
slab

15c BUTTONHOOK
ROUTE

15a KERN KNOTTS
CRACK

15b INNOMINATE
CRACK

16: TOPHET WALL (S+) 80m

Summary: A long route with some awkward moves. Stupendous positions and rock scenery put it high amongst the greats.

First Ascent: Harry Mills Kelly and R.E.W. Pritchard, July 1923 (Direct Start added by Michael de Selincourt, August 1925.)

Best Conditions: South-east facing at 850m. Dries quickly.

Approach: As for Route 15 to Kern Knotts, then follow the Gable Traverse – a narrow path that makes a slightly rising traverse westwards across the south face of the mountain. Just prior to reaching the crag the path crosses Great Hell Gate, a vast scree run. Turn off up the scree to gain the foot of the huge wall on the left – Tophet Wall. GR:211 019. 1hr 10mins. Alternatively, use the Gavel Neese approach (refer to Route 18).

Starting Point: Just to the right of the lowest point of the wall is a diagonal crack which slants to the right. Gain this from the right.

Descent: At the top a narrow ledge is encountered. Follow this to the right and then descend steeply to the scree (M).

Tophet Wall is a truly amazing climb and its ascent should be a landmark in any climber's career. It is certainly one of Kelly's finest, though it is impossible to pick the best when the competition includes Moss Ghyll Grooves and Rib and Slab.

Kelly began a serious examination of the route in 1920 and did a considerable amount of exploration and gardening before he felt it would go. Even then he did not include the present first pitch, although he had already climbed most of it on a rope from above. Three years later a Fell & Rock Club team were gathered below the wall discussing the possibility of a direct start when de Selincourt, a non-member, soloed it in front of their very noses. Sadly their comments are not on record!

This start is hard, on rock which is very steep and rather too smooth. More worrying still is the little black wall at the beginning of the next pitch. There are no runners here, just a profusion of misleading and sweat-polished holds, none of them the longed-for jug, and all of them sloping the wrong way. On the stance above, one gladly swaps difficulty for exposure.

Thereafter the route is pure joy; great slabs and spires of gloriously ragged rock with holds like handlebars and nought but air and a firm grip to keep you from the scree. Kelly and Pritchard celebrated with strawberries at the top, and though few of us come so well prepared these days, it certainly is *that* sort of route.

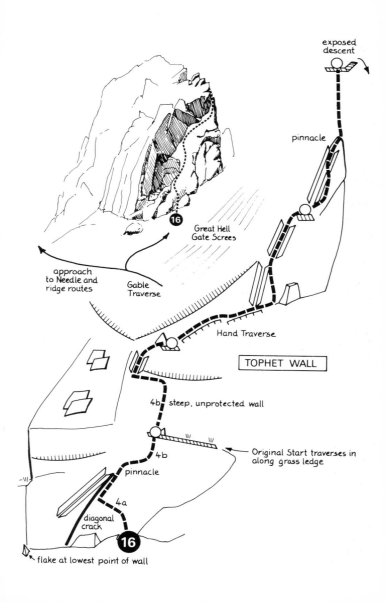

exposed
descent

pinnacle

Great Hell
Gate Screes

16

approach
to Needle and
ridge routes

Gable
Traverse

Hand Traverse

TOPHET WALL

4b steep, unprotected wall

4b

Original Start traverses in
along grass ledge

pinnacle

4a

diagonal
crack

16

flake at lowest point of wall

17: NAPES NEEDLE (VD+) 20m

Summary: A tiny and much loved peak of great historical interest.

First Ascent: Wasdale Crack – Walter Parry Haskett Smith, June 1886. Lingmell Crack – Owen Glynne Jones, Mrs Commeline and Norman Collie, April 1892. The Arête – Henry Fowler, September 1894.

Best Conditions: South facing at 800m. Quick to dry.

Approach: As for Route 15, then follow the Gable Traverse, a narrow path across the south face of the mountain. Just past the vast scree run of Great Hell Gate a vaguer track strikes up steeply to the foot of the Needle. GR:211 019. 1hr 10mins. Alternatively, use the Gavel Neese approach (refer to Route 18).

Starting Point: The Wasdale Crack and The Arête start at the foot of a polished off-width on the Wasdale Face. Traverse round right on ledges for the Lingmell Crack.

Descent: By abseil or down-climbing.

Having had his appetite whetted by a brief glimpse of the Needle through swirling mist and rain (some things never change), Haskett Smith returned a few years later with his usual climbing partner, John Robinson. They 'threaded the Needle', passing between it and the Napes, and then ascended Needle Ridge, albeit avoiding the harder sections.

Two years later, finding himself at a loose end one afternoon, Haskett Smith casually completed an amazing *tour de force*. First he climbed Central Gully on Gable Crag – the first ascent up that cliff – then descended Needle Ridge proper (finding it 'quite feasible'), despite being encumbered by a long fell-pole. This brought him to the foot of the Needle. He climbed to the shoulder by the Wasdale Crack, which he found to be choked with turf and stones. From here the summit was, as he wrote later, 'only two blocks away'. The final moves he considered 'a nervy proceeding' and he made good use of a small handhold a foot or so below the lip. This handhold is still as critical as ever, and if the moves to reach it are less lichenous than they were a century ago, they have certainly become more polished. But at least you should have fewer problems than Haskett Smith did in getting down again.

The ascent of the Needle was far more than just a bold climb. Its singular appearance fired the public imagination, and it was made the subject of numerous magazine articles and photographs, all of which served to attract potential mountaineers to the Lake District. Haskett Smith has quite rightly been hailed as the father of British rock climbing.

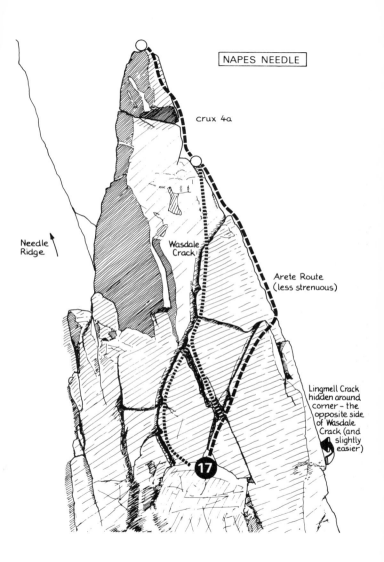

NAPES NEEDLE

crux 4a

Needle Ridge

Wasdale Crack

Arete Route (less strenuous)

Lingmell Crack hidden around corner – the opposite side of Wasdale Crack (and slightly easier)

17

18: (a) Needle Ridge VD 110m
(b) Arrowhead Ridge Direct VD 80m

Summary: Two well-situated ridges which have proved continuously popular.

First Ascent: Needle Ridge – Walter Parry Haskett Smith and John Robinson, September 1884 (lower pitches added by Arthur Woodhead, Stanley Jeffcoat and John Laycock, January 1911). Arrowhead Ridge Direct – A.G. Topham, Horace Walker and Cecil Slingsby, March 1896 (the ordinary route – 1892).

Best Conditions: South facing at 800m. Very quick drying.

Approach: Refer to Route 17. A more direct (but less pleasant) alternative from Wasdale is via Gavel Neese, the south-west shoulder of Great Gable. Leave the Styhead track just after a footbridge crosses Gable Beck and follow a steep path on the left. On reaching the scree the path goes by Moses' Finger (a conspicuous boulder) and joins the Gable Traverse. Go rightwards along this to reach the crags. GR:211 019. 1hr.

Starting Point: Needle Ridge starts at a short slab in the gap between Napes Needle and the main face. To reach Arrowhead Ridge first traverse left from the Needle to the 'Dress Circle', the wide ledge under the start of Eagle's Nest Ridge. Now follow the path left across grass to the next ridge which has a prominent tower, the Arrowhead, low down. Start at the lowest point of the ridge. (Note: left again is an even more outstanding pinnacle, the Sphinx.)

Descent: At its top, Needle Ridge turns sharp left. A descent can be made down right from here to the screes of Great Hell Gate. Alternatively, follow the ridge leftwards to its very end (ignoring tempting turn-offs). Descend from here, either down the scree ahead, or via a vague gully system between the Arrowhead and Sphinx Ridges.

Arrowead Direct: good geriatric rock, as Harry Griffin would have it; a description ably illustrated by Horace Walker, a contemporary of Whymper's, who was around 70 when he made its first ascent. But children of ten have been seen on these climbs, so youth is no barrier.

Needle Ridge, being more committing, is the finer. And though the first polished slab is hard, it is on the upper section that the exposure begins to exert its wrench-like grip. By contrast, Arrowhead eases off quite rapidly and almost fades into the hillside. But this doesn't seem to matter, and the memory of those exciting moves over the Arrowhead itself, and the stretching stride that follows, linger to call one back again and again, hopefully until well past retirement age.

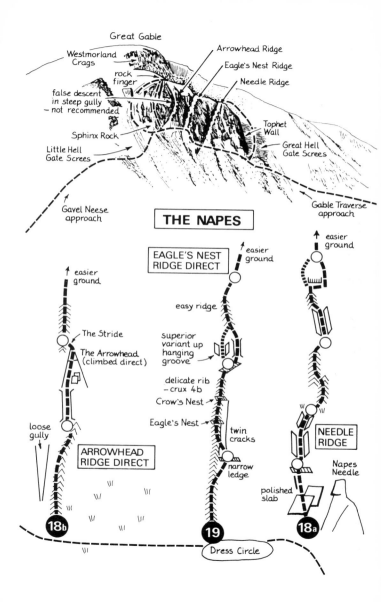

Great Gable

Westmorland Crags

rock finger

Arrowhead Ridge

Eagle's Nest Ridge

Needle Ridge

false descent in steep gully – not recommended

Sphinx Rock

Little Hell Gate Screes

Tophet Wall

Great Hell Gate Screes

Gavel Neese approach

Gable Traverse approach

THE NAPES

↑ easier ground

EAGLE'S NEST RIDGE DIRECT

↑ easier ground

↑ easier ground

↑ easier ground

The Stride

The Arrowhead (climbed direct)

easy ridge

superior variant up hanging groove

delicate rib – crux 4b

Crow's Nest

Eagle's Nest

twin cracks

loose gully

ARROWHEAD RIDGE DIRECT

narrow ledge

NEEDLE RIDGE

Napes Needle

polished slab

18b

19

18a

Dress Circle

19: EAGLE'S NEST RIDGE DIRECT (VS–) 100m

Summary: A very exposed route with the most tenuous moves at the top. Traditionally graded *VS* due to the lack of protection, although nowadays a good wire can be placed just above the Crow's Nest. (Illustrated on Route 18 diagram.)

First Ascent: Godfrey Solly, William Cecil Slingsby, G. Phillip Baker and William Brigg, April 1892.

Best Conditions: South facing at 800m. Dries quickly in summer.

Approach: Refer to Routes 16 and 18.

Starting Point: From Napes Needle traverse left for 20m or so to the Dress Circle, a good viewpoint for the Needle. Eagle's Nest Ridge rises directly above.

Descent: Follow an easy continuation ridge to a juncton with a ridge which crosses at right-angles. Follow this leftwards, ignoring tempting turn-offs, to its very end. Descend from here, either down the scree ahead, or via a vague gully system between the Arrowhead and Sphinx Ridges.

Eagle's Nest Ridge Direct was an outstanding lead of the Victorian age and its first ascensionists remained in awe of what they had accomplished. Solly himself later confessed that 'no inducement would ever have tempted me to go up again without a rope from above.'

At the time there were just three other routes on the crag, and it was whilst engaged on one of these that Solly and Slingsby observed that 'above the little platform, the ridge was continued at a less severe angle, and that there appeared to be three steps or pitches that were possibly less difficult than the lower part.' Solly rued, 'Time has shown that our conclusion was arrived at too hastily'!

Incidentally, the name of the climb has little to do with ornithology, but derived from the party's opinion of their leader's comical appearance as he sat astride the tiny ledge above the first step. From there Slingsby gave him a shoulder to the Crow's Nest, but he was on his own on the crux where he found retreat impossible, and proceeded 'with the knowledge that if even one hand or foot slipped all would be over.' It is these last moves, made on a series of small and sloping holds, that ensure the route maintains its reputation to this day. Modern protection methods are of scant assistance and any fluttering of the limbs which might escalate into flight should be immediately curtailed.

Tophet Wall (Route 16).
  (Climber: Stephen Reid. Photo: Steve Ashton.)

20: ENGINEER'S SLABS (VS) 60m

Summary: A stupendous route, possessing an atmosphere out of all proportion to its size. Best done within the mountaineering tradition by continuing to Gable's summit.

First Ascent: Frederick Graham Balcombe, Jack Shepherd and C.J. Astley Cooper, June 1934.

Best Conditions: Being north facing at 900m makes this an unfortunately wet crag. Allow at least a week of dry weather.

Approach: (1) From Honister. As for Route 49, but follow the fence, southwards, and cross the second stile to the summit of Grey Knotts. From there a track leads over Brandreth and Green Gable to Windy Gap (the col between Great and Green Gables). A path contours rightwards under the crag. (2) From Borrowdale or Wasdale. Follow approaches for Route 15 to the northern end of Styhead Tarn. Climb Aaron's Slack, a red, scree-filled open gully to the west, to Windy Gap. Many other approaches are possible. GR:212 105. 1hr 15mins.

Starting Point: Follow the path rightwards under several buttresses until a vast smooth wall is seen high above. Engineer's Slabs takes the central crack-line in this wall, starting just left of a mossy chimney. It can be reached by an unpleasant scramble up grass on the right or, better, by climbing Sledgate Ridge (S+).

Descent: Well left of the crag, by a path descending to Windy Gap.

Graham Balcombe astonished the small climbing scene of 1934 with a series of brilliant ascents achieved after only a few short holidays in the Lakes. Every new route in Wasdale that wet summer was his. The Direct Finish to Central Buttress and Buttonhook Route were the hardest, but it was Engineer's Slabs that gained the biggest reputation. Twenty years passed before it was repeated.

Despite the exposure, the lower pitches seem simple enough now with good runners and reasonable belays. Imagine them without either and the flavour of those pre-war days begins to return. The final V-chimney is the nub. Usually slimy, it leaves one with a feeling of profound respect for a leader who recommended that (as there was no belay below it) subsequent parties should carry up their own chockstone.

Meteors last only an instant before their glory fades. The reasons for their departure are as varied as the reasons for their success. In Balcombe's case he took to potholing, going on to pioneer that elite sport within the world of dangerous sports – cave-diving. It takes all sorts.

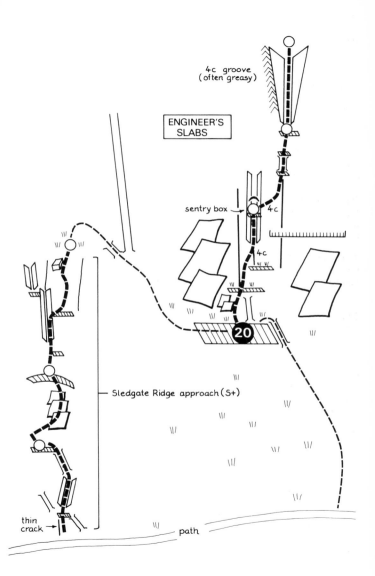

4c groove
(often greasy)

ENGINEER'S
SLABS

sentry box → 4c

4c

Sledgate Ridge approach (S+)

20

thin
crack

path

Ennerdale

There are a great many crags in Ennerdale, and some of them are very good, but all lie in the shadow of the magnificent Pillar Rock.

The valley, which is dominated by commercial forestry, is virtually devoid of human habitation and, since the closure of the Ennerdale road, all approaches to Pillar are arduous.

These climbs are long, and a multiplicity of lines and ledges means that route finding can be a problem, especially when the mist rolls in. This is also true of the descents; all but one of the obvious gullies are impassable. The rock is sound and rough when dry, but, as on any unfrequented crag, the odd loose block is not unknown. A high level of mountaineering competence is required to climb safely on Pillar Rock.

Approaches: 1 From Ennerdale: Cars are not normally permitted beyond Bowness Knot on the northern shore of Ennerdale Water. From the car-park, continue up the valley to Gillerthwaite by a rather dreary forestry track. (Permits to motor this section are available from the B.M.C., current price £1. Write, enclosing an S.A.E., to Colin Wornham, Dower Cottage, Pardshaw Hall, Cockermouth, Cumbria.) Continue on this track for about 2km, then fork right over the River Liza. Turn left and then, after 50m, follow a good path which ascends diagonally through the forest to the crag. GR:173 124. 1hr 30min.
1a There is a very infrequent bus service from Whitehaven to Ennerdale Bridge (Thursdays and Fridays only), from where lanes and footpaths can be followed around the southern shore of Ennerdale water.
2 From Buttermere: Take the path from Gatesgarth Farm (GR:194 150) to Scarth Gap (GR:189 134). Leave the main track after a slight descent on the Ennerdale side to follow a poorly defined path that leads round to the right, some way above the forestry plantations. This soon becomes more obvious and descends gently through the conifers to the valley bottom. Go downstream to cross the River Liza by a footbridge. Follow the forestry road downstream, fork left, then leave this track after 20m to follow a steeply ascending ride through the forest to a stile. Follow the west bank of the stream up to the crag. 1hr 30min.
3 From Wasdale: Take the good track to Black Sail Pass (GR:192 116) then branch off north-west along the ridge of Looking Stead towards Pillar Mountain. Just before the ridge steepens, a cairn on the right marks the start of the High Level Route to Pillar Rock via Robinson's Cairn. 2 hrs.

Accommodation: *Camping:* Limited camping at farms at the lower end of the valley (some of which also do bed and breakfast).

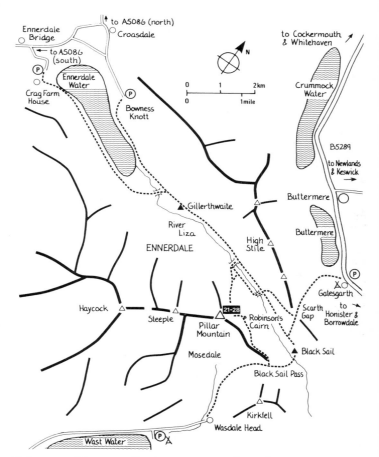

High camps/bivouacs: Creatures great and small make the forest unsuitable unless entomology is a keen interest. There is a good stream near the Rock, but only a few flat sites.

Youth Hostels: Black Sail (GR:195 124) and Gillerthwaite (Cat Crag) (GR:142 141). Both are closed from November to mid-March.

Services: At Ennerdale Bridge there is a pub and a cafe as well as small shops. The nearest garages are at Cleator Moor and Whitehaven.

Rib and Slab (Route 25b).
  (Climber: Alistair Hopkins. Photo: Stephen Reid.)

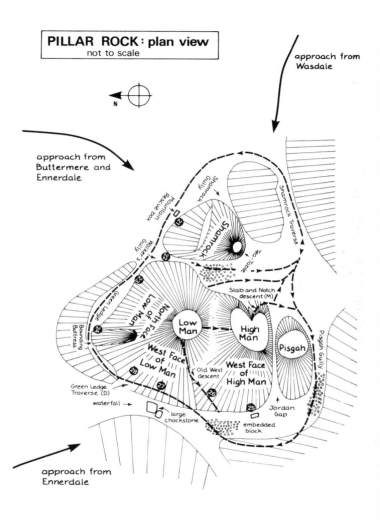

PILLAR ROCK: plan view
not to scale

N

approach from
Wasdale

approach from
Buttermere and
Ennerdale

Mountain Rescue box

Walker's Gully

Green Ledge

Shamrock Gully

Shamrock

Shamrock Traverse

Tan-Trod

Slab and Notch descent (M)

North Face of Low Man

Bounding Buttress

Low Man

High Man

Pisgah

West Face of Low Man

West Face of High Man

Old West descent

Green Ledge Traverse (D)

waterfall →

large chockstone

embedded block

Jordan Gap

Pisgah Gully

approach from
Ennerdale

21: **THANATOS/ELECTRON (HVS) 170m**

Summary: This worthwhile combination of routes makes a good introduction to the harder climbs on Pillar (and not just because the start is easy to find!). Short, well-protected cruxes and rambling link pitches give climbing more reminiscent of the early 1950s than the mid-1960s.

First Ascent: Electron – Geoff Cram and Chris Eilbeck, September 1966. Thanatos – Bill Lounds and Eilbeck, May 1968.

Best Conditions: North facing at 650m. The main pitch of Electron dries slowly and is considerably harder when wet. Allow at least a week of dry weather, except perhaps in late summer.

Approach: Refer to the area introduction and plan of the Rock for initial approaches. The north face of the crag is split by the dark cleft of Walker's Gully; the area to the left of this is the Shamrock. A blue Mountain Rescue box provides a useful landmark.

Starting Point: A little to the right of the Mountain Rescue box, below a prominent capped corner. (Refer also to Route 22 diagram.)

Descent: From the Tea-Table, skirt the top of Shamrock Gully and scramble up to the Shamrock Traverse. Follow this interestingly exposed path back down to the left. (Alternatively, to reach the West Face climbs, traverse it rightwards and descend the Pisgah Gully.)

The exposure on Thanatos creeps up on you slowly, the corner absorbing all interest until your head fetches against the roof and the only way out is left. That's when it hits you (the exposure, that is, not the roof). From here on every inch of ground is hard won and unreasonable obstinacy for once becomes a desirable trait.

Beyond the terrace, the crux bulge of Electron's groove succumbs to delicate bridging on sloping holds – unpleasant if wet. A fine problem, but the penultimate pitch proves better: a magnificent off-width crack that can only be climbed elegantly by layback. As on CB's Great Flake, there are no distractions or excuses to be found after the comforting chockstone runner at the start. Fortunately the holds are brilliant.

It all ends at the 'Tea-Table', a unique and suggestively named feature of uncertain stability.

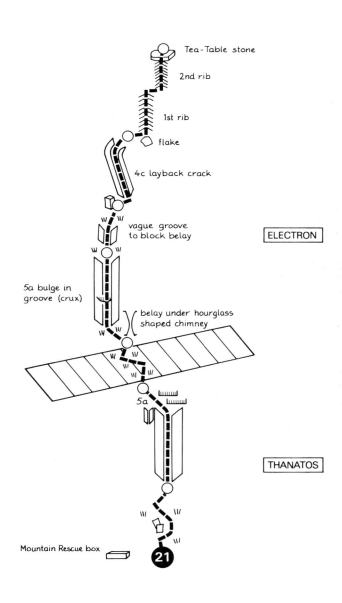

Tea-Table stone

2nd rib

1st rib

flake

4c layback crack

vague groove
to block belay

ELECTRON

5a bulge in
groove (crux)

belay under hourglass
shaped chimney

5a

THANATOS

Mountain Rescue box

21

22: WALKER'S GULLY (S+) 140m

Summary: An outstanding gully climb, marred only by the risk of stonefall from the scree slopes above. Steep and sustained, with the most strenuous obstacle saved until last.

First Ascent: Owen Glynne Jones, George Abraham and Alfred Ernest 'Ginger' Field, January 1899 (the Broadrick brothers climbed the Direct Start during a failed attempt in September 1898).

Best Conditions: North facing at 650m. Can be climbed in all weathers but seldom comes into true winter condition. Helmets are advisable and the route is best attempted when there are few people about.

Approach: Refer to the area introduction and plan of the Rock for initial approaches. Walker's Gully is the great dark cleft which splits the northern side of the Rock, separating Shamrock from Low Man.

Starting Point: At the Gully.

Descent: Scramble up to the right, avoiding steep scree, to join the Shamrock Traverse. Follow this back down to the left (exposed); or, to reach the West Face climbs, traverse it rightwards and descend Pisgah Gully. Alternatively the ridge on the left provides a further 60m of pleasant climbing at D standard to Shamrock's summit.

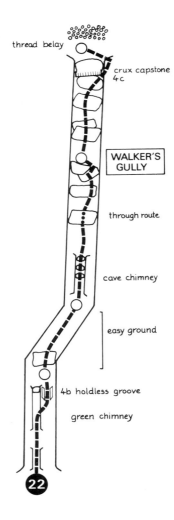

thread belay

crux capstone
4c

WALKER'S
GULLY

through route

cave chimney

easy ground

4b holdless groove

green chimney

22

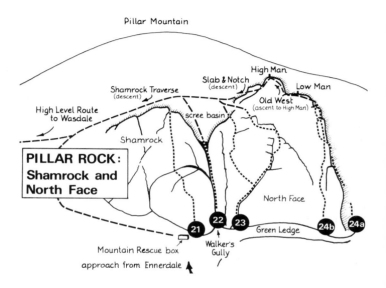

Pillar Mountain

High Man

Slab & Notch
(descent)

Low Man

Shamrock Traverse
(descent)

Old West
(ascent to High Man)

High Level Route
to Wasdale

scree basin

Shamrock

**PILLAR ROCK:
Shamrock and
North Face**

North Face

Green Ledge

21   22   23   24b   24a

Mountain Rescue box

Walker's
Gully

approach from Ennerdale ▲

'Summer has set in with its usual severity', wrote Samuel Taylor Coleridge, poet, opium addict and an early explorer of the fells. He was not the first, and most certainly will not be the last, to bemoan the climate that gives the Lake District its Lakes. A century later, George Abraham recorded the conversation of a complaining visitor; 'Does it do anything but rain here?' 'Yaas!' answered a local, 'It sometimes snows!' Luckily this is one route where conditions matter little to either enjoyment or success – though a dry sense of humour should be considered essential.

The first ascent of Walker's, the culmination of many previous attempts, was an extraordinary epic conducted in icy but thawing conditions. At the final chockstone, Jones kindly removed his boots before standing on his second's head and battling to the top in stockinged feet. When hauling up his jacket, a spare pair of socks fell out of a pocket. 'It gave us quite a shock at the time,' he later recorded, 'for we thought it was a packet of sandwiches.' It was Jones's last major lead in the Lakes: later in the year, this outstanding pioneer of his age was killed in a fall from the Dent Blanche.

23: (a) North Climb (VD+) 110m
(b) North-East Climb (VD+) 140m

Summary: Big holds, comfortable stances, and historical problem pitches give these climbs a tweedy feel. They are among Pillar's easiest, and all the more enjoyable for that.

First Ascent: North Climb – Walter Parry Haskett Smith, Geoffrey Hastings and Cecil Slingsby, July 1891 (Dr Joseph Collier and S.B. Winser climbed the Nose in 1893). North-East Climb – George and Ashley Abraham, April 1912 (C.F. Stocks, Miss Capper, Claude Worthington and Joseph Gaspard climbed the upper pitches in May 1912).

Best Conditions: North facing at 650m. The current F&RCC guide reminds us that North Climb is 'traditionally done by a large jolly party in wet weather'. North-East would be foul in such conditions. Allow four dry days.

Approach: Refer to the area introduction and plan of the Rock for initial approaches. To the right of Walker's Gully, the major gully on the northern side, the path rises steeply for a few metres to the start of Green Ledge.

Starting Point: Near the start of Green Ledge, below a ledge at head-height on the face. (Refer also to Route 22 diagram.)

Descent: From the finish of either route, make a rising traverse left across grassy ledges to enter the top of the scree basin above Walker's Gully. Descend as for Route 22 via the Shamrock Traverse.

North Climb was nine years in the making and, when it parted suddenly with one of its many unsecured boulders, very nearly cost Haskett Smith his life. Even then he was defeated by The Nose and had to be lowered into Savage Gully to finish; a variation he later disparaged as 'stooping to conquer'. Although the route without The Nose is only D+, this classic 'boulder problem in the sky' should not be missed, for it is no more terrifying than the final few feet of Napes Needle, or the difficult crack on Bowfell.

North-East, a later and lesser route, warrants inclusion for its fine outlook and clever route finding. Less polished than its more famous neighbour, it seems more adventurous. The ghosts of the Abraham Brothers encourage you at every hold.

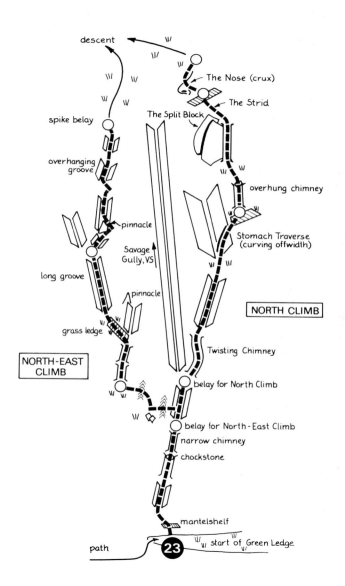

24: (a) North-West Climb (VS–) 140m
(b) Megaton (HVS+) 140m

Summary: Long and varied, these two routes make the best use of the vast North Face. Pitches are sustained and route finding is tricky. Good rock and outstanding positions.

First Ascent: North-West Climb – Fred and Arthur Botterill, Lehmann Oppenheimer and Dr James Taylor, June 1906 (Robertson Lamb, W.L. Collinson, R. Horton and Everard Wilfred Steeple climbed Lamb's Chimney in August 1906). Megaton – Bill Young and William 'Barney' Barnes, May 1972.

Best Conditions: North facing at 650m. Allow at least four dry summer days.

Approach: Refer to the area introduction and plan of the Rock for initial approaches. Traverse Green Ledge rightwards to the curved Bounding Buttress.

Starting Point: Refer to the diagram opposite. (Refer also to Route 22 diagram.)

Descent: From the summit of the Low Man descend via the Old West as for Route 27. Alternatively, continue by a well worn climb (M) to the High Man and descend Slab and Notch as for Route 25.

Camping at Pillar is highly recommended: make a lazy supper by a babbling brook whilst others stumble homeward in the dusk, then rise with the lark and catch Megaton at its best – warm in the morning sun.

A slight pitch serves well to gear the mind from sleeping-bag to waking crag. A good thing at this early hour, because the slab that follows comes frighteningly close to *E1*. But a stance is to hand, and those fortunate enough to have had a tight rope on the slab can now take the lead for some energetic bridging up a magnificent bottomless groove. An easier groove above is followed by one of the most exhilarating chimney-cracks you will ever find. It delivers the well organised early riser to a splendid breakfast site on the summit of the Low Man.

North-West Climb is altogether a simpler proposition, though in its day it was considered a remarkable breakthrough and George Abraham thought it 'much too difficult to become either useful or popular.' It too can be climbed to advantage in the morning but, better still, it provides a fine end to the day as the sunset gilds the ripples on distant Ennerdale Water.

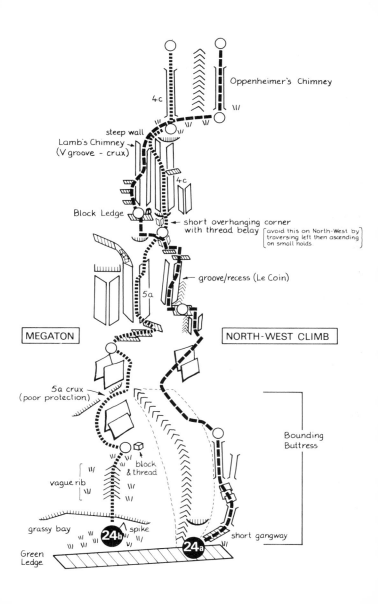

Oppenheimer's Chimney

4c

steep wall

Lamb's Chimney
(V groove - crux)

4c

Block Ledge

short overhanging corner
with thread belay
[avoid this on North-West by
traversing left then ascending
on small holds]

groove/recess (Le Coin)

MEGATON

NORTH-WEST CLIMB

5a

5a crux
(poor protection)

Bounding
Buttress

block
& thread

vague rib

grassy bay

24b spike

24a

short gangway

Green
Ledge

25: (a) New West Climb (D+) 100m
(b) Rib and Slab Climb (S) 100m

Summary: New West is a route of unending superlatives; exposed, inescapable, and of a consistently high standard. Rib and Slab is of similar quality.

First Ascent: New West – George and Ashley Abraham, Dr J.H. Wigner and Claude Barton, May 1901. Rib and Slab – Claude Holland, Harry Kelly and Colin 'Ferdie' Crawford, July 1919.

Best Conditions: West facing at 650m. Allow at least three dry days.

Approach: As for Route 26.

Starting Point: About 10m down from the Jordan Gully, below the West Face, a large block lies embedded in the scree. New West starts just below this block; Rib and Slab some 10m further left, under a small, tilted paddock. (Refer also to Route 27 diagram.)

Descent: Via Slab and Notch. First locate the gully that cuts into the east side of the summit of the High Man. Descend the gully for a few metres until polished holds lead to a rib on the right (all directions are given as if looking out). Descend the rib to a ledge. Follow the ledge to the right, until above a steep corner. Descend the corner to a large slab which is crossed to the right to easy ground near the Jordan Gap. Alternatively an abseil may be made into the Jordan Gap.

The passage of countless pilgrims has so polished the holds of the New West that they gleam like stone flags in some ancient cathedral. But this should be no surprise on such a brilliant climb, the inspiration of the famous 'Keswick brothers'. Their dedication to photography, particularly during their frequent climbs with O.G. Jones, has left us with a unique record of rock climbing in its infant years. They made their ascent of New West shortly after Jones's death, accomplishing the traverse to the foot of the difficult chimney by facing outward and sidling along a grass ledge. Since then, sufficient holds have been revealed for it to be climbed in a more conventional manner, although it still demands, in George Abraham's words, 'care and coolness'. Without doubt it is the finest climb on the Rock. Even the superb Rib and Slab suffers slightly by comparison, assuming the unlikely guise of a modern eliminate.

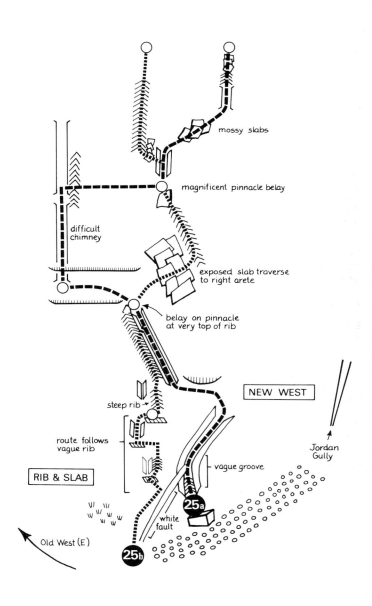

mossy slabs

magnificent pinnacle belay

difficult chimney

exposed slab traverse to right arete

belay on pinnacle at very top of rib

NEW WEST

steep rib

route follows vague rib

Jordan Gully

vague groove

RIB & SLAB

25a

white fault

25b

Old West (E)

26: (a) Gomorrah (VS) 85m
(b) Vandal (VS+) 85m

Summary: Although shorter than many climbs here, these natural corner lines have a big, open feel that gives considerable cause for agoraphobia.

First Ascent: Gomorrah – Harry Mills Kelly and Claude Holland, August 1919 (Bill Young and Roelof Schipper climbed the Direct Start in June 1967). Vandal – Geoff Oliver, John Cheesmond and Len Willis, June 1959.

Best Conditions: West facing at 650m. The grooves may remain greasy early in the season. Allow four dry days in summer.

Approach: Refer to the area introduction and plan of the Rock for initial   approaches.   When approaching   from   Ennerdale, ascend well to the right of the waterfall and scramble up scree below the West Face. Otherwise approach   via   the   Shamrock Traverse and Pisgah Gully, or by the Green Ledge Traverse (M) from the Mountain Rescue box (not recommended if wet).

Starting Point: Scramble up the Old West for a few metres (refer to Route 27 diagram) until under the prominent low overhang of Vandal. Gomorrah begins up the vague rib well to the left and down from this, whilst Vandal starts with a short grassy pitch leading to a belay in the groove under the overhang. (Refer also to Route 27 diagram.)

Descent: As for Route 25.

Kelly and Holland had trouble on Gomorrah, the second of two new routes tackled that day. Holland's disintegrating plimsolls were the cause of it, thoughtlessly failing to stick when passing the roof. The resulting swing, loss of his pipe, and glancing blow on the head from a dislodged stone, did not improve his temper and he maintained a brooding silence throughout the long walk back to Wasdale. There, to Kelly's surprise, he voiced his considered opinion that the climbs should be called Sodom and Gomorrah. But the suggestion was too controversial for the F&RCC, and for many years they were known simply as Routes 1 and 2.

Though more sustained, Vandal is not really much more technically difficult than many of Kelly's routes; yet, surprisingly, it and Goth were the first new routes on Pillar in almost twenty years. In those days when blank rock was still abundant, Oliver had picked the lines by the simple expediency of filling in the gaps in Heaton Cooper's crag diagrams – gaps that provide nerve-racking exposure on all but the calmest days.

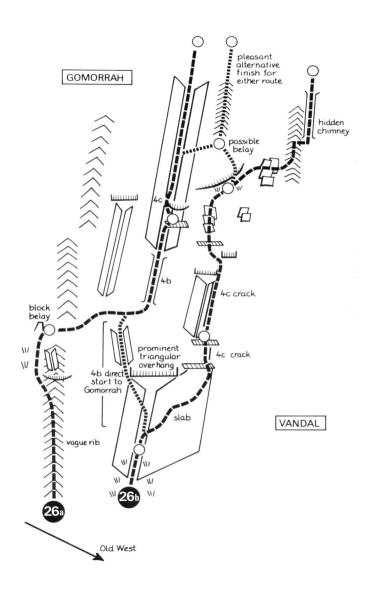

GOMORRAH

pleasant
alternative
finish for
either route

hidden
chimney

possible belay

4c

4c crack

block belay

4b

4c crack

prominent
triangular
overhang

4b direct
start to
Gomorrah

4c crack

slab

VANDAL

vague rib

26a

26b

Old West

27: WEST WALL CLIMB (VD) 70m

Summary: A fine, safe route on excellent rock. Magnificent situations.

First Ascent: Harry Mills Kelly, Claude Holland and Colin 'Ferdie' Crawford, July 1919.

Best Conditions: West facing at 650m. Allow two dry days.

Approach: Refer to Route 26 for approaches and to the diagram opposite for location of the Old West. From the foot of the Old West, descend the scree until a few metres above a huge jammed boulder where a waterfall issues from the slope. Traverse left on grass ledges until in a line directly above this boulder.

Starting Point: Scramble up to the start of the first pitch – a short wall leading to a ramp.

Descent: The route finishes near the top of the Low Man, on the well worn scramble of the Old West. Follow it down to the right (looking in) to emerge on the scree below the West Face of High Man. Alternatively, continue by the Old West (M) to the summit of High Man. Descend from here via Slab and Notch as for Route 25.

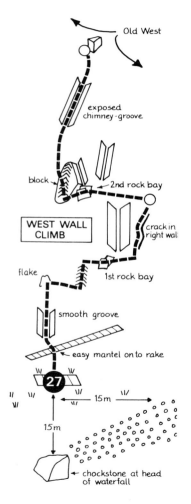

Old West

exposed chimney-groove

block

2nd rock bay

WEST WALL CLIMB

crack in right wall

flake

1st rock bay

smooth groove

easy mantel on to rake

27

15m

15m

chockstone at head of waterfall

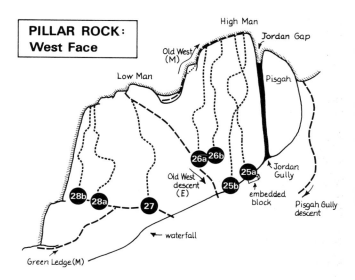

PILLAR ROCK: West Face

High Man
Jordan Gap
Old West (M)
Low Man
Pisgah
26a 26b
25a
Jordan Gully
Old West descent (E)
25b
embedded block
Pisgah Gully descent
28b 28a
27
waterfall
Green Ledge (M)

In 1919, Kelly would have prepared for his lead of West Wall Climb by tying a hemp rope around his waist and shouldering a length of cord. A strong advocate of rubbers, he is likely to have worn plimsolls instead of the more usual nailed boots. In fact, choice of footwear was subject to a debate as heated as that concerning bolts today; many considered that use of rubbers was not playing the game as they 'did not give the rocks a chance'!

There were few advances in equipment over the next twenty years. Threading inserted chockstones was tolerated, but pitons were frowned on, and, although karabiners were in use on the Continent as early as 1910, they were seldom seen in Britain until the Second World War. Running belays, where they existed, generally involved tying the threaded cord directly around the rope (permissible with hemp which does not melt).

Dangerous run-outs on these early climbs were minimised by reducing pitch lengths wherever possible. West Wall Climb, for instance, was originally climbed in eight pitches. Any further security was achieved by judicious application of the golden rule: *the leader must not fall!*

28: (a) Appian Way (S+) 70m
(b) Goth (E1) 90m

Summary: The West Face of Low Man is noted for its good rock, absence of grass ledges, and speed of drying. These routes are representative of the best on the face.

First Ascent: Appian Way — Harry Kelly and R.E.W. 'Appie' Pritchard, 1923. Goth — Maurice Felix de St Jorre and Neville Hannaby, June 1959.

Best Conditions: West facing at 650m. Although the face is quicker drying than others on Pillar, the rock is still greasy if wet. Allow two dry summer days.

Approach: As for Route 27 to grass ledges above the jammed boulder of the waterfall, then traverse more or less horizontally left over further grass ledges for about 30m to a large block on a terrace.

Starting Point: Appian Way starts from the large block. Goth starts a few metres down to the left, at the right-hand and vaguer of twin grooves separated by a hanging arête. (Refer also to Route 27 diagram.)

Descent: As for Route 27.

It is easy to dismiss Appian Way and Goth as just two more Pillar routes, yet either one of them would be the star of any lesser crag.

Appian Way includes such a variety of features that it seems unfair to highlight any particular section. But certainly the layback crack and subsequent wall traverse on the first pitch rate highly. Deciphering the correct line on the wall is both crucial and entertaining.

By contrast Goth condenses so much into the twenty feet of the crux arête that the remainder is inclined to blur. Highly exposed, it catches the slightest breeze and the struggle up an overbearingly steep wall (where hairline cracks reluctantly accept only the tiniest of wires) is not made easier by the ensuing battle with a wind-whipped anorak. Of course St Jorre didn't have the option of worrying about wires during the first ascent — they had yet to be invented. But confident from an early repeat of Cenotaph Corner, his rope billowed out in a graceful curve as, crouched on the shelterless stance, Hannaby lost his cap to a mischievous zephyr.

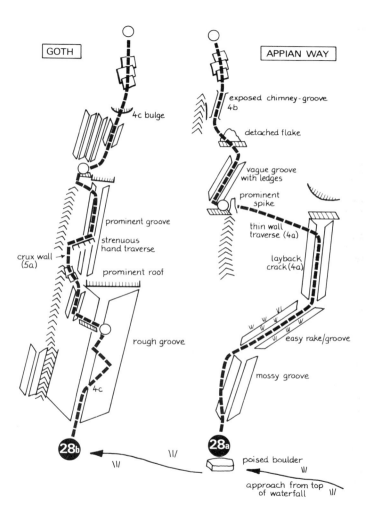

GOTH

APPIAN WAY

4c bulge

exposed chimney-groove
4b

detached flake

prominent groove

vague groove
with ledges

strenuous
hand traverse

prominent
spike

crux wall
(5a)

thin wall
traverse (4a)

prominent roof

layback
crack (4a)

rough groove

easy rake/groove

mossy groove

4c

28b

28a

poised boulder

approach from top
of waterfall

Buttermere

Buttermere possesses a haunting beauty that is reward enough for those who take the trouble to reach it. And though perfect ridges and peaceful waters make this area a favourite of the rambling fraternity, it is largely ignored by climbers. But the climbing here is good; be it the sunny ease of Grey Crags, the sombre north face of Eagle Front, the compact classics of High Crag or the less than compact ones of Buckstone How. There has to be a catch, and there is: the routes are always a little further, or a little slower to dry, or a little longer than those of comparative playgrounds in other dales. And of course, for most people, it takes longer to get here. But those who persevere will not regret it, and they may well find themselves, like others before them, bypassing more fashionable and better known venues in order to return here time after time.

Approaches: For those travelling from the east all roads lead through Keswick, from where the B5289 makes a pleasant but often exasperatingly slow drive through Borrowdale to Seatoller and the Honister Pass. Alternatively, stay on the A66 for a few miles beyond Keswick to Braithwaite and then take the spectacular road over Newlands Hause to Buttermere village. In winter both ways may be blocked, but the Whinlatter Pass (B5292), also gained from Braithwaite, is usually open. This descends to the Cockermouth–Lorton Vale–Buttermere road (B5289).

When approaching from the west, turn right off the A5086 at Lamplugh Cross for Loweswater and eventual junction with the B5289. There is a summer bus service to Buttermere Village from Keswick. An alternative is to take a bus from Keswick to Seatoller and walk up to Honister Pass.

Accommodation: *Camping*: Limited camping at Gatesgarth (GR:195 150), the highest farm up the valley, and at Dalegarth (GR:187 159). *Youth Hostels*: Buttermere (GR:178 168) and Honister Pass (GR:225 135). *Hotels*: There are two in Buttermere village (closed during winter) and there are other bed and breakfast places in the valley.

Services: Both hotels in Buttermere serve meals. The nearest shop is at Lorton, several farms sell milk and eggs. For most supplies, including climbing gear, a trip to Keswick is necessary.

Winter Climbing: Newlands Hause Waterfall (III) (GR:193 176) and drainage from old mines on the Honister flank of Fleetwith Pike (mainly IV or V, GR:217 140) provide reliable water-ice in a good freeze. Birkness Gully (III/IV) and Birkness Chimney (III/IV), at the far left of Eagle Crag (*see* Route 30).

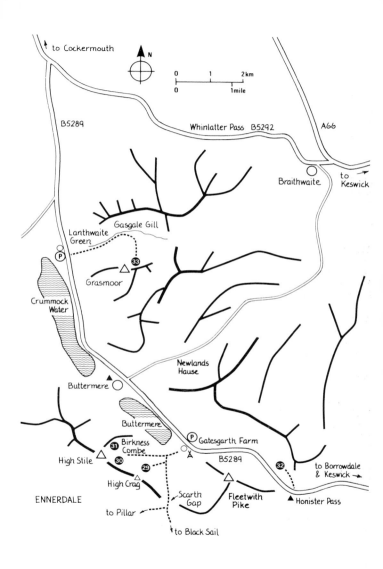

29: HIGH CRAG CLASSICS

(a) Delilah (VS) 55m
(b) High Crag Buttress (HVS) 65m
(c) Philistine (E1) 60m (d) Samson (HVS) 55m

Summary: Four exceptional routes on perfect rock. Protection is excellent on all except Philistine (good only on the harder sections).

First Ascent: Delilah – Bill Peascod and Brian Blake (via the right arête), August 1951. High Crag Buttress – Jeff Allison and Les Kendall, September 1962 (with one point of aid; climbed free by Paul Nunn and Pat Fearnehough on second ascent). Samson – Kendall (unseconded), October 1962 (by the direct route, using aid; climbed free, via the traverse, by Kendall and Arthur Clarkson, May 1963). Philistine – Ed Cleasby and Bill Birkett, June 1975.

Best Conditions: Though north facing at 450m, all except Samson dry quickly. Allow one breezy summer day (three for Samson).

Approach: Park near Gatesgarth Farm on the B5289 (this is the highest farm up the valley at GR:194 150). Follow the footpath through the farmyard and up the hillside, taking the left-hand branch as far as a gate (200m). Follow the fence tiresomely up to the crag, which is easily identified by the Goblin's Eyes of High Crag Buttress (GR:183 145). 30mins.

Starting Point: Delilah – a short way up Gatesgarth Chimney, which bounds the crag on its right side. High Crag Buttress – directly below the twin caves of the Goblin's Eyes. Samson and Philistine – at a short, greasy chimney below the central arête of the crag.

Descent: To the left of the crag by a precarious path leading to down-climbing – nasty in the wet.

Geoffrey Winthrop Young was one of several early Birkness explorers who stayed at Hassness, Professor Pigou's home on the shore of Buttermere. But his ascent of Gatesgarth Chimney in 1913 was an isolated event, and it was Bill Peascod who took the first real interest in High Crag. Delilah was Peascod's best route, but with his departure for Australia the 'Cinderella Valley' resumed its enchanted slumber.

Les Kendall was next on the scene. With Jeff Allison he climbed the Buttress and then made an epic, aided ascent of Samson in pouring rain. As darkness encroached, the ropes became hopelessly jammed and with cramped hands he was forced to hack through them with his peg hammer before soloing the greasy upper slabs.

Philistine, the finest climb on the crag, was inexplicably overlooked – much to the joy of a later generation.

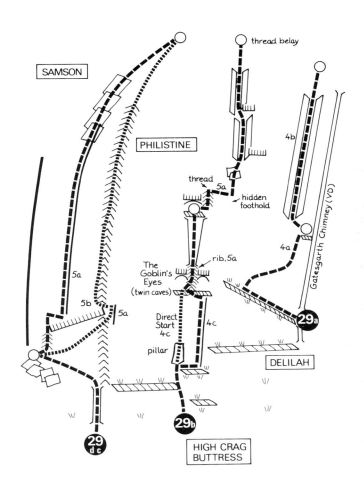

30: EAGLE FRONT (VS) 165m

Summary: An acknowledged classic, with fine positions and a high level of exposure. Perseverance is required to obtain good belays.

First Ascent: Bill Peascod and Bert Beck, June 1940

Best Conditions: North facing at 700m. Slow to dry and much harder when greasy. Allow at least a week of dry weather.

Approach: Park near Gatesgarth Farm on the B5289 (this is the highest farm up the valley at GR:194 150). Follow the footpath through the farmyard and up the hillside, taking the right-hand branch. Continue along the path to gentler ground, crossing a wall by a stile. Finally follow a stream up the combe to the crag (GR:172 145). 45mins. (Note: Birkness Combe is marked Burtness Combe on some maps.) The small buttresses across scree to the right are Grey Crags.

Starting Point: At a vague, grassy rib, 7m left of a point where the main face meets the scree fan of the descent gully.

Descent: By the loose gully to the right of the crag.

Hanging high above Buttermere is Birkness Combe and standing tall within the Combe is Eagle Crag. From its summit the views are of the sort that stir the soul. One suspects that it wasn't merely ease of access from Maryport that brought Peascod here time and time again.

Peascod was a miner and, like his contemporary Jim Birkett, the forerunner of a new phenomenom, later typified by Brown and Whillans – the working-class climber. During the 1940s he was responsible for virtually every new route in Buttermere, Eagle Front being one of the earliest.

He climbed the route in one push, cleaning from the bottom and on the nerve-racking second pitch he had only one poor sling runner. Even today that pitch is not well protected, and the slightest drizzle quickly turns an ascent of its sloping holds into an epic. But it is the next few feet that provide the most difficulty. Some consolation, as you struggle, to know that Peascod exclaimed here, 'Look out, I'm off any moment!'

Beyond the terrace, delicate climbing leads to a comfortable perch in an eagle's eyrie of a belay below a corner crack (plainly visible from the combe below). It is impressively vertical, but as Beck noted, it has, 'good sharp handholes in it and good flat footholds beside it.' It was, he recalled, the only place where they found either.

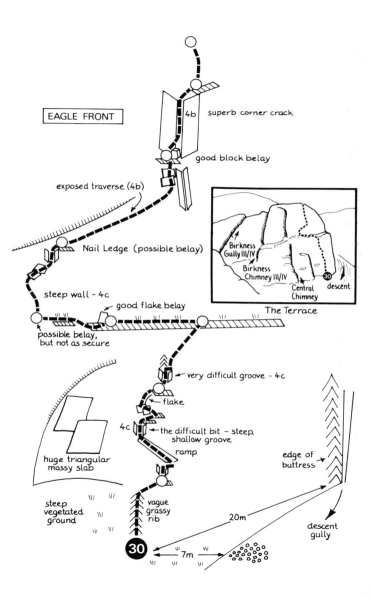

EAGLE FRONT

4b   superb corner crack

good block belay

exposed traverse (4b)

Nail Ledge (possible belay)

steep wall - 4c

good flake belay

possible belay,
but not as secure

Birkness
Gully III/IV

Birkness
Chimney III/IV

Central
Chimney

30   descent

The Terrace

very difficult groove - 4c

flake

4c   the difficult bit - steep,
shallow groove

ramp

huge triangular
mossy slab

edge of
buttress

steep
vegetated
ground

30   vague
grassy
rib

20m

descent
gully

7m

31: GREY CRAG

(a) Mitre Buttress Direct (VD) 75m
(b) Suaviter (S) 45m (c) Fortiter (VS) 50m
(d) Oxford and Cambridge Direct (VD+) 40m
(e) Dexter Wall (VS+) 40m

Summary: Excellent rock, a sunny aspect, and short pitches make this a popular place for beginners – despite the long walk.

First Ascent: Oxford and Cambridge – Herbert Reade and party, September 1914 (direct variations – unknown). Mitre Buttress Direct – Arthur Cecil Pigou and party, July 1915. Dexter Wall – Bill Peascod and Bert Beck, March 1941. Suaviter and Fortiter – Peascod and Beck, July 1941.

Best Conditions: South-east facing at 750m. With the exception of Fortiter, all the climbs dry very quickly.

Approach: As for Route 30. The buttresses lie across scree to the right of Eagle Crag (GR:172 147). 1hr. (Note: Birkness Combe is marked Burtness Combe on some maps.)

Starting Point: Refer to diagram opposite.

Descent: Refer to diagram opposite.

Lehmann Oppenheimer's book *The Heart of Lakeland* gave Buttermere an early popularity which accounted for much of the attention bestowed here prior to the First World War. Both the routes included from this period are quite delightful; a succession of surprise holds (on the roughest of red rock) make for easy work over very steep ground. But there was plenty of scope left for Peascod, and the remaining routes are his – including the hardest, Dexter Wall. This, the only climb he top-roped prior to leading, must have been an awesome undertaking in 1941. Even today the protection is none too comforting for those last few groping moves where every hint of a good hold turns out to be a blind crack.

Wilfred Noyce once said, 'Too much of Grey Crags after an army diet is like champagne on indigestion.' Luckily military fare is much improved these days, and those who over-indulge themselves here are left with nothing worse than a surfeit of effervescent sparkle.

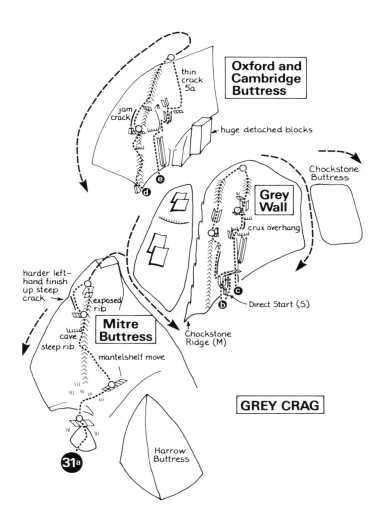

Oxford and Cambridge Buttress

thin crack 5a

jam crack

huge detached blocks

e

d

Grey Wall

crux overhang

Chockstone Buttress

c

b

Direct Start (S)

Chockstone Ridge (M)

harder left-hand finish up steep crack

exposed rib

cave

steep rib

Mitre Buttress

mantelshelf move

31a

Harrow Buttress

GREY CRAG

32: (a) Cleopatra (HVS) 80m
(b) Honister Wall (S+) 95m
(c) Sinister Grooves (VS) 85m

Summary: While none of these climbs is technically hard, the doubtful, slaty rock takes some getting used to and they are graded accordingly. Protection is generally adequate, though care should be taken with the final belays.

First Ascent: Sinister Grooves – Bill Peascod and Bert Beck, March 1946. Honister Wall – Peascod and Beck, May 1946. Cleopatra – Peascod and Brian Blake, May 1951.

Best Conditions: West facing at 500m. The crag is very quick-drying and though Cleopatra may retain some wet streaks, the actual climbing mostly avoids them.

Approach: Park in the car-park behind the Youth Hostel at the summit of Honister Pass. Cross the road and follow a disused quarry ramp northwards. At the end of the ramp cross scree and drop down and round to the foot of the crag at GR:223 143 (note: crag position is marked too far north-west on some maps). 10mins.

Starting Point: Cleopatra starts at a shattered pinnacle that almost touches the centre of a long, low roof which guards access to the first really continuous area of rock encountered on the approach. Honister Wall begins about 20m to the left, where a squat, blocky pinnacle is separated from the cliff by a large jammed chockstone. Sinister Grooves starts some 10m left again at a wide, open groove containing twin cracks.

Descent: An easy ramp leads down right. It is very loose.

Buckstone How, black as Guinness or Cooper's Oxford Marmalade, is not everyone's cup of Earl Grey. Even Jim Birkett, who had worked at Honister Pass quarries, never considered it as a climbing ground. Not surprising really: the crag looks loose and forbidding, and, to be honest, first appearances are not deceptive. Peascod was the first to examine it seriously, and he was duly rewarded with a series of fine routes.

Insecure rock apart, Buckstone How has a lot going for it. It dries fantastically quickly – as fast as Shepherd's – and is only a few minutes' easy walk from the pass. Also, the established climbs are virtually clean of doubtful holds (though it could be foolish to stray far from the correct line). Moreover, the routes are long for a roadside crag and, with a gaunt aspect over the upper Buttermere Valley and the impressive decay of the old mineworkings, the whole place has more than its fair share of 'atmosphere'. It is that which makes this a crag for the connoisseur.

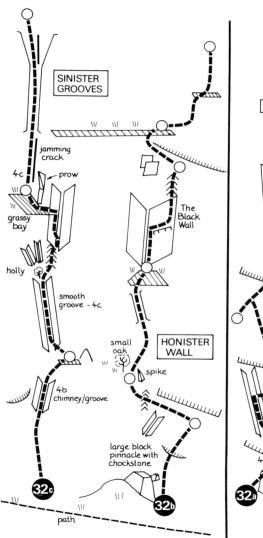
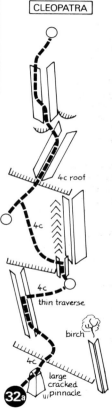

SINISTER GROOVES

jamming crack

4c

prow

grassy bay

holly

smooth groove - 4c

4b chimney/groove

32c

path

HONISTER WALL

The Black Wall

small oak

spike

large block pinnacle with chockstone

32b

CLEOPATRA

4c roof

4c

4c thin traverse

birch

4c

32a large cracked pinnacle

Suaviter (Route 31b).
 (Photo: Stephen Reid.)

Dove Crag Gully (Route 33).
  (Climber: Walter Phipps. Photo: Stephen Reid.)

33: DOVE CRAG GULLY (IV/V) 100m

Summary: A unique ice experience with two contrasting main pitches, both steep and technical. Ice-screw protection.

First Ascent: Unknown.

Best Conditions: Despite being north-east facing at 800m, a prolonged thaw-freeze period of at least a week is required for good ice to develop on the Direct. The first pitch is especially slow to form. The Chicken Variation is more often in condition.

Approach: From the B5289, Buttermere to Cockermouth road, at Lanthwaite Green (GR:159 208). Park near the telephone kiosk.

Follow a path eastwards along Gasgale Gill until the south side of the valley opens out considerably. Minor crags to the south are passed at first, but Dove Crag is unmistakably huge (though not well seen from the beck). It is reached by tiring scrambling up grassy slopes. GR:179 205. 1hr 15mins.

Starting Point: At the left-hand side of the crag in a deep cleft. If there is no ice on the left wall of the cleft it can be avoided by traversing in to the snow basin from the left.

Descent: To the left of the crag.

Dove Crag Gully in good conditions is a waterfall frozen in time. Great stalactites of clear blue crystal splay out in all directions before plunging dagger-like into the belly of a deceptively simple snow basin. The eye, drawn immediately to all this gaudy splendour, is apt to overlook the murky grotto underneath, and it is only on entering its cavernous portal that any true sense of scale is achieved.

Right from the start iron teeth must confront vertical ice, but behind you the rapidly closing walls soon become comfortably chimneyable. A perilous squeeze round the chockstone roof brings the snow basin to hand, knee and clenched foot.

Ascending steep water ice is a trusting business, and the best climbers are devout believers. For them the merest nick suffices for ice-axe or crampon. The sane, however, will insist on solid placements, plenty of ice screws, and treat every hairline crack as a potential dinner-plate. While commendable for peace of mind, this approach applied to Dove Crag Gully will guarantee exhaustion. Thankfully a convenient icicle hidy-hole provides a chilly rest before the final gleaming bulge.

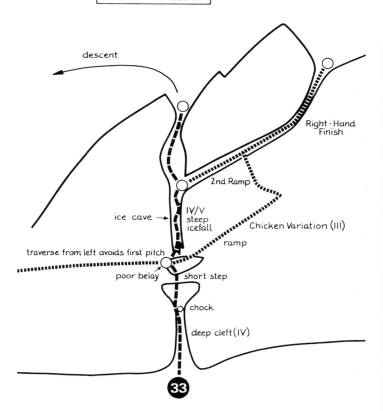

DOVE CRAG GULLY

descent

Right-Hand
Finish

2nd Ramp

ice cave →

IV/V
steep
icefall

Chicken Variation (III)

ramp

traverse from left avoids first pitch

poor belay   short step

chock

deep cleft (IV)

33

Borrowdale

Borrowdale is very much the climber's valley, boasting numerous cliffs of all shapes, sizes and qualities. Most routes are within easy walking distance of the road, and both the lurexed crag-rat and the dayglo outdoor education group are much in evidence. But don't let this put you off; most crags are worth at least one visit, and all the climbs described, although lacking high mountain grandeur, possess individual character. Indeed, many are routes of national renown.

Parking can be troublesome in summer, unless one is willing to walk along the road for a few minutes from one of several car-parks in the valley. The weekend climber should also be prepared to queue for popular classics such as Little Chamonix and Troutdale Pinnacle. An early or midweek start solves both these problems.

The weather is generally better here than elsewhere in the Lakes, and it is often possible to climb in sunshine on Falcon or Shepherd's while storm clouds surge around higher summits.

Approaches: Most people will travel down the B5289 from Keswick, which is easily reached from the M6 via the A66 (junction 40). From the west, Buttermere and Honister Pass give access to the southern end of the valley. There is a good bus service from Keswick during the summer, and a more limited one in winter.

Accommodation: *Camping:* Borrowdale is extremely well served with campsites. These will be found at Derwentwater (GR:261 232) and Castlerigg Hall (GR:282 225), near Keswick, and further down the valley at Ashness Farm (GR:059 684), which is handy for Falcon, Gowder and Shepherd's. Hollows Farm, Grange (GR:249 166), is best for Black, Great End Crag and Goat, while Chapel House Farm, Longthwaite (GR:257 140), Stonethwaite Farm (GR:266 134), Seatoller Farm (GR:254 137) and Seathwaite Farm (GR:236 122) are all reasonably close to the other crags.
Youth Hostels: Keswick (GR:267 236), Barrow House (GR:268 200), Longthwaite (GR:255 143) and Honister Pass (GR:225 135).
Hotels: There is a climber's bunkhouse in Keswick (Trekkers Lodge, telephone Keswick 72267) and hotels and guest houses both in Keswick and throughout the valley. Many close down over winter.

Services: Restaurants in Keswick, Seatoller and in hotels, and many cafes. The major climbers' pubs are The Packhorse and The Dog and Gun in Keswick. Keswick has many shops, including Fisher's – a mountaineer's department store. Also several garages. 24 hour petrol at Penrith.

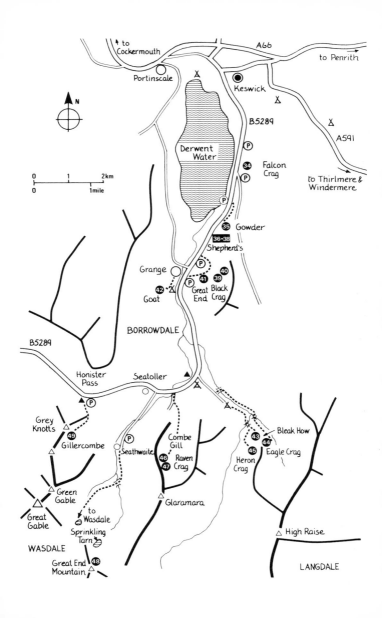

34: (a) The Niche (E2) 60m
(b) Dedication (E1) 55m

Summary: The Niche is an absolutely brilliant climb, wending a powerful but intricate route up the impressive central section of the Lower Crag. Protection is good when the going gets tough, but is best described as 'thought provoking' on the easier bits. Dedication is low in its grade; the long main pitch provides a good measure of ability for any aspiring extreme leader.

First Ascent: The Niche – Ado Liddell and Ray McHaffie, August 1962. Dedication – Paul Ross and Eric Metcalfe, May 1957.

Best Conditions: West facing at 200m. Slow to dry after heavy rain. Allow four dry days.

Approach: From Keswick take the B5289 along Borrowdale. Turn left towards Watendlath and pull in to the car-park immediately after the junction. A path from the back of the car-park leads to the Lower Crag. GR:271 205. 5mins.

Starting Point: The Niche starts at the foot of a bulging wall directly under the huge niche in the centre of the crag. Dedication begins about 7m to the right.

Descent: To the left of the crag.

The Niche – now there lay a challenge if ever there was; not only to gain it, but to leave it and its comfortable falcon's eye view over Derwent Water. The call was answered by Ray McHaffie, who in the early 1960s was making the first advances in a long-lasting love affair with Borrowdale, during which he would unearth over a hundred new climbs. The Niche, one of his earliest and on which he and Liddell alternated leads, is the grandest by far.

The Niche: horror on a hot day, as dry mouth and sweaty fingers combine to hinder the 'it's-only-two-so-go-for-it' moves of the old tension traverse to gain its cool haven. The Niche: of no rest for there's more, tip-toeing delicately under roofs and past old aid pegs, their controversy faded with disuse. The Niche: forgotten in the frantic search for good holds that have to be somewhere in the groove beyond. The Niche: way below now and almost over, but puzzling still in its final runnerless wall. The Niche: a name that lingers, each move etched firmly in the memory of the challenge.

Dedication, by contrast, is a good climb for those who prefer brains to brawn. Confidence is required to believe that holds will be found the full length of the slab (and science to find them), but once embarked on, the moves flow together. The end arrives all too soon.

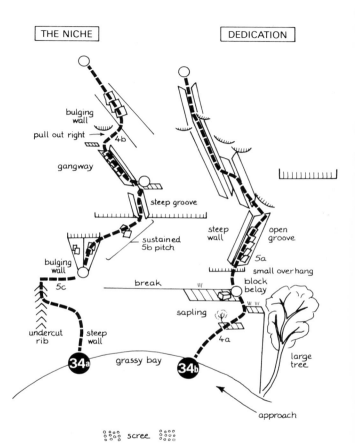

THE NICHE

DEDICATION

bulging wall

pull out right → 4b

gangway

steep groove

sustained 5b pitch

bulging wall
5c

undercut rib

steep wall

34a

grassy bay

steep wall

open groove

5a

small overhang

break

block belay

sapling

4a

34b

large tree

approach

scree

35: FOOL'S PARADISE (VS) 120m

Summary: A varied route up an impressive piece of rock. The climbing and situations make up for the odd doubtful section. Protection is poor on the second pitch.

First Ascent: Pat Vaughan and J. Dennis Wildridge, April 1951.

Best Conditions: West facing at 200m. Best avoided on warm sunny days for reasons outlined below. Allow two dry days.

Approach: There is no parking worth speaking of near to the crag, and it is best to use Kettlewell car-park about 1km (½ mile) to the north (this is the first car-park on the right after leaving Keswick on the B5289). Cross the road into the woods opposite, from where a pleasant path runs parallel to the road and eventually joins the well-trodden Lodore Falls path. Follow this to the falls and the crag. The path under the crag is very popular in summer and great care must be taken with loose masonry. GR:266 187. 5mins from the road. 15mins from the car-park.

Starting Point: Start at the lowest point of the buttress, below and slightly right of a clean-cut rib.

Descent: Via an open gully on the left of the crag.

Spare a thought for the National Trust when, still grumbling about lack of car-parks, you pass their small iron sign at the entrance to Gowder Woods. The National Trust's particular paradise just happens to include almost every crag of importance in the Lakes and, even to a real fool, it is plain that climbers are in their debt.

The crag is not far from the gate, and should you find yourself here on a hot summer's day, you will soon discover why this climb merits its name — the place will be swarming with ants. So come back instead in crisp October when the oaks and beeches are all shades of gold, the skies are clear blue, and mist hangs like dragon's breath on Derwent Water. Scrunch up through the woods on a rustling brown carpet to find the moss on the lower pitches as dry as dust.

Most folk reckon the traverse to be the highlight of the climb, and it must be one of the most photographed pitches in the valley with its background of woods, sombre lake and distant hills. Easy posing on easy slabs make for a cheerful and spectacularly situated grin. But the difficulties are greater and peculiarly grinless above; bulges and vertical grooves in the main, until a final chimney ends the climb as suddenly as it began, in a horizontal world of autumnal colour.

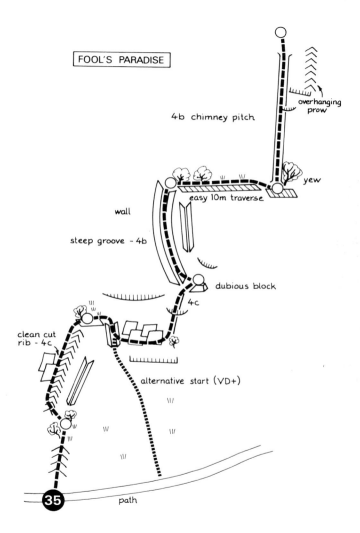

FOOL'S PARADISE

4b chimney pitch

overhanging prow

yew

easy 10m traverse

wall

steep groove - 4b

dubious block

4c

clean cut
rib - 4c

alternative start (VD+)

35

path

36: (a) Little Chamonix (VD) 75m
(b) The Bludgeon (E1) 60m

Summary: Two tremendously exciting routes with testing finales. The finish of the Bludgeon involves climbing an overhanging bulge on doubtful jugs (it sheds the odd one now and then) and is probably the most lowered off route in the Lakes.

First Ascent: Little Chamonix – Bentley Beetham, May 1946. The Bludgeon – Paul Ross and Peter Lockey, April 1957.

Best Conditions: West facing at 150m. The upper sections of both routes dry quickly, but their first pitches may remain damp for a while after heavy rain.

Approach: Refer to Route 37.

Starting Point: Locate a slight bay under the central area of the right-hand (Chamonix) buttress. (Immediately left of this the path dips down a little below a smooth wall and then rises across scree to the central buttress.) On the left of the bay is a large pinnacle, in the middle a blunt slabby arête, and on the right a short crack with a leftward-slanting groove above. The Bludgeon starts at the blunt arête. Little Chamonix at the crack.

Descent: Follow a narrow path left until it joins a track leading downwards.

These routes have more than neighbourliness in common. Both final pitches – albeit at either ends of the grading scale – involve arm-sapping reaches for holds that could hardly be bigger. But if only there wasn't so much space beneath!

Little Chamonix, the solo creation of Bentley Beetham, is one of the most popular climbs in the valley, and as such it has received the kind of treatment climbers reserve for the very best-loved of pitches. It has been climbed up and down, in winter, in Alpine boots, by torch-light, combinations thereof, and even, believe it or not, in boxing gloves and roller skates.

A wide groove forms a good first pitch that gives way suddenly to a short scramble through woods. A second groove goes easily as far as a large polished block, but then one must almost throw oneself off this to reach miniscule holds on the right wall. Thereafter a fine *à cheval* position accesses a possible stance. At first glance there now seems no way out that isn't *HVS* at least. But if you stare for long enough at the overhanging wall above then jugs will begin to materialise. A few heart-in-mouth swings should see you safely to the Belvedere.

The Bludgeon was the sadistic inspiration of that other outstanding Borrowdale climber – Paul Ross. It has yet to be done in boxing gloves and roller skates.

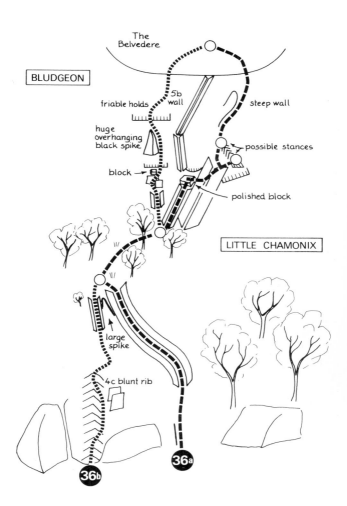

The
Belvedere

BLUDGEON

friable holds

5b
wall

steep wall

huge
overhanging
black spike

block

possible stances

polished block

LITTLE CHAMONIX

large
spike

4c blunt rib

36a

36b

37: ARDUS (S+ or VS) 40m

Summary: A nicely varied route in which three contrasting pitches build up to an exciting finale on the steep left wall.

Other climbs at a similar or easier standard will be found on Brown Slabs, situated on the right-hand end of the left-hand buttress. The lines are either obvious or inconsequential.

First Ascent: Ardus – Vince Veevers, Horace 'Rusty' Westmorland and P. Holt, May 1946 (Short Notice – Dennis English and Bill O'Hara, August 1960; Direct Finish – unknown).

Best Conditions: West facing at 150m. Unlike most of the Shepherd's routes, the deep crack of Ardus can remain damp for days after rain. This does not make it unclimbable, just slightly more awkward.

Approach: From Keswick follow the B5289 along Borrowdale, past Falcon Crags to the Lodore Hotel. The crag, hidden by woods, is on the hillside on the left about 40m past the hotel. It may be approached directly from below or by a path that slants left from a farm to the south. Unfortunately the nearest car-park is about 1.5km (1 mile) back up the road towards Keswick. At less busy times, and in winter, there are a few parking spaces just south of the crag near the Borrowdale Hotel. The crag is formed by three buttresses; Ardus takes the enormous slabby groove that bisects the central one. GR:264 185. 2mins.

Starting Point: The groove, in its lower section, has two branches forming an inverted V. Start under the left-hand branch.

Descent: A cautious descent can be made down the blocky gully to the right of the buttress. Otherwise descend to the left of the crag.

The laid-back groove of Ardus positively beguiles you into action simply by comparison with its towering flanks. Innumerable sloping holds on sloping slabs later, and one feels like an insect poised on the edge of a Venus Fly Trap. You want to stop but you can't – it's so good.

The corner hardly gives in gracefully either, but at least it has runner placements. However, 10m of strenuous polished crack is enough to convince you that the Direct Finish ahead is not for first-timers. Danger signals start to flash but a line of holds across the slab on the left seduces you like nectar. Fly on the wall. The trap has sprung.

In later years – when experience has taught you not only how to feel comfortable on walls but how to walk upside down on the ceiling – Short Notice will set your antennae trembling.

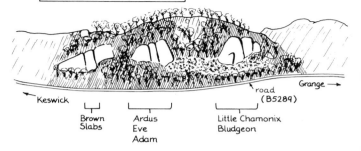

SHEPHERD'S CRAG

Keswick ←   Grange →

road (B5289)

Brown Slabs

Ardus
Eve
Adam

Little Chamonix
Bludgeon

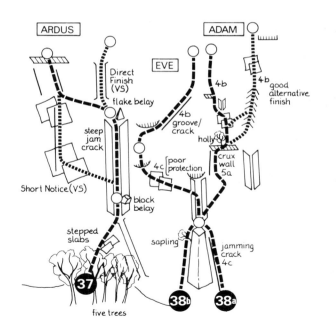

ARDUS

Direct Finish (VS)

flake belay

steep jam crack

Short Notice (VS)

stepped slabs

37

five trees

EVE

ADAM

4b

4b good alternative finish

4b groove/crack

holly

crux wall 5a

4c poor protection

block belay

sapling

jamming crack 4c

38b   38a

38: (a) Adam (VS+) 45m
(b) Eve (VS) 55m

Summary: An idyllically matched pair of climbs, perfectly set in a little Rock Garden of Eden. Eve involves a serious traverse over difficult slabs and so is not a good route for beginners to second. (Illustrated on Route 37 diagram.)

First Ascent: Eve – Bill Peascod and Brian Blake, August 1951. Adam – Paul Ross and Ray Wilkinson, August 1955.

Best Conditions: West facing at 150m. Both routes dry very quickly.

Approach: Refer to Route 37.

Starting Point: To the right of the groove of Ardus is a complex wall with a large block pinnacle in a little bay at its lower right-hand side. Adam starts up the jamming crack on the right-hand side of this pinnacle. Eve takes the vaguer groove on its left.

Descent: A cautious descent can be made down the blocky gully to the right of the buttress. Otherwise descend to the left of the crag.

Adam picks a fight with you immediately. Chivalry or chauvinism? Subdue him with aggressive jams and footwork, and he merely catches you off balance with a slippery finger-crack and then forces you to mantelshelf into a holly. Sorer (and perhaps wiser) you become cautious on the upper section. Just as well, considering the lack of gear.

Eve is altogether more feminine, entry to her rocky delights being fiercely guarded by a sharp groove. And then, once attained, the false promise of apparently soft and yielding slabs is revealed; the moves are virtually protectionless. A typically perilous seduction.

The apple in your lunch-box hardly seems adequate reward.

'Borrowdale is the heart of the finest scenery and the best climbing in England.' Walter Parry Haskett Smith, *Climbing in the British Isles* (1894).

'Haskett Smith . . . Haskett Smith,
  Alone he slew the monolith.'
    George Basterfield, *Mountain Lure* (1947).

39: THE MORTICIAN (HVS) 110m

Summary: After a fingery start to steep grooves, the climb rises from the trees by some interesting jamming to a fine finish on the pinnacle. Well protected. (Illustrated on Route 40 diagram.)

First Ascent: Brian 'Bomber' Thompson and William 'Barney' Barnes, August 1969.

Best Conditions: West facing at 350m. The grooves are slow to dry. Allow three days after heavy rain.

Approach: Follow the B5289 south from Keswick, passing Falcon and Shepherd's Crags, until about 1.5km (1 mile) beyond the Borrowdale Hotel. Here a private track branches left (east) at a sharp bend; park in a lay-by on the main road just south of this point, return to the track, and follow it into an open field. The crag lies ahead up a wooded slope (GR:263 172). 20mins.

Starting Point: Just left of the lowest point of the crag, at the foot of a slab to the left of a wide crack behind an old fallen tree.

Descent: To the right via an exposed footpath, or, safer, walk directly back from the cliff edge and then go right.

Of all the climbs on Black Crag, The Mortician, a direct line up the highest part of the cliff, is a firm favourite. The real climbing starts with the second pitch, the first few moves of which usually cause the most trouble. Here a slip of a roof, barely more than a bulge really, bars the way to a smooth, inviting groove. The first problem is to find a way of overcoming *Extreme* technical difficulties at the roof. The good protection helps. Leaders regularly get stuck here and yo-yo up and down until the slab above bristles with wires. 'I'll just have a rest and then go up and have another look' is a commonly heard refrain. The holds are tiny, and even after surmounting the barrier it is hard to remember exactly how. There's little time for reminiscence anyway: the second crux looms – an awkward transfer to a steepening crack on the right. Some comfort to know that its degree of cruciality is inversely proportional to one's jamming ability!

The next pitch shown on the diagram is in fact part of another climb, but this bold and brilliantly placed finger traverse is far more entertaining than the true line. And if you think it is all over at this point then it must be a long time since you climbed Troutdale Pinnacle.

40: TROUTDALE PINNACLE (S−) 125m

Summary: The best roadside (well, almost) route in the Lakes, with excellent rock and continuously interesting climbing. Its only drawback is its popularity. The final pitch is the crux and is considerably exposed. Confident ropework is needed on the traverse.

First Ascent: Fred Mallinson and Ralph Mayson, May 1914.

Best Conditions: West facing at 350m. Dries quickly. Allow a day after heavy rain.

Approach: Refer to Route 39.

Starting Point: Just left of the lowest point of the crag, at a wide crack in a corner behind an old fallen tree. The crack leads to a ledge within 4m. A similar crack 5m to the right leads to the same point.

Descent: To the right via an exposed footpath, or safer walk directly back from the cliff edge and then go right.

What a climb this is − each pitch perfectly arranged and positioned (think of reassembling them in reverse order if you doubt it). But then classic status is not so much the result of predictable formulae as of popular opinion, and on Troutdale Pinnacle the climbers have voted with their feet. It shows in the polished holds.

Most of the old classics include a thrutchy off-width crack, but at least this one has the sense to get it over with at the start. From then on there is little to swear at. Delightful slabs unfurl and lead to an excellent block stance, from where the climbing assumes a more serious nature. Long reaches over a bulge gain a smooth black groove. At its top a tiny and precarious belay is guaranteed to provide an interesting experience for those not leading through, and perhaps explains why the climb is so popular with young men introducing young ladies to the pleasures of the layaway and the good jam.

A downward traverse must now be made over the following slab. This is not particularly difficult, but the amount of dislodged protection left dangling on the rope when it is taken in tight shows up the subtle difference between a mere leader and a good leader.

The final pitch is not only the best, the steepest, and the most exposed, but it is also the most difficult. Its finishing move is the hardest of all. Success, or failure, will be found at your fingertips.

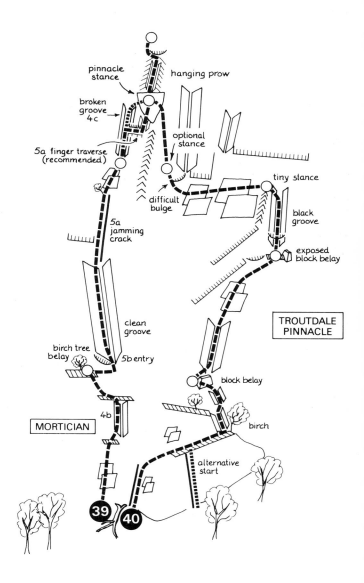

pinnacle stance

hanging prow

broken groove 4c

5a finger traverse (recommended)

optional stance

difficult bulge

tiny stance

5a jamming crack

black groove

exposed block belay

clean groove

TROUTDALE PINNACLE

birch tree belay

5b entry

block belay

MORTICIAN

4b

birch

alternative start

39 40

41: (a) Great End Corner (HVS) 80m
(b) Banzai Pipeline (HVS+) 100m

Summary: Two of the longest climbs in the valley. Both are nicely continuous at their standard, but Banzai Pipeline possesses a short groove at the end of the second pitch which is technically a full grade harder. Protection is available, but dependent on having the appropriate chock – a good selection should be taken. Being fairly recent in origin, neither route is free from moss or doubtful rock. Helmets advised.

First Ascent: Great End Corner – Dave Nicol, Colin Downer, Ian Conway and Dave Hellier, April 1975. Banzai Pipeline – Nicol, Downer, Howard Cobb and Chris Bacon, June 1977.

Best Conditions: North facing at 300m. Mossy – allow three dry days after heavy rain.

Approach: Not to be confused with Great End Mountain. Approach as for Black Crag (Route 39) to the open field. Then follow a path on the west of the stream and cross a wall (gate). Contour to the right through steep woodlands (no path). GR:259 170. 20mins.

Starting Point: The crag is formed by two walls that meet at an obtuse angle in the centre. Great End Corner starts at the foot of this corner. Banzai Pipeline starts at a small pinnacle near the lower end of the left wall.

Descent: By poor paths to left or right.

In the late 1970s two Borrowdale 'cragrats' were burrowing away at a newly 'discovered' but vegetated crag which had already provided them with the classic Great End Corner. They were cleaning a line to its left when Downer, armed with the essential ice-axe and wire brush, began to jumar up one of the ropes Nicol had left in place overnight. At 15m he was overcome by a horrible sinking feeling and in the nick of time grabbed the disapearing end of the 'other' rope as it started pulling round the belay! Luckily his grip was strong and shortly afterwards Banzai Pipeline was weeded into being.

A decade on and it seems as though that prolonged and enthusiastic battle with nature was in vain; all but the best routes are gradually being re-submerged under gallons of enveloping greenery. Fortunately our two are well-trodden enough to remain reasonably clean, though even on Bank Holiday weekends it is not unusual to have them to yourself while across the valley blinkered queues form under Praying Mantis.

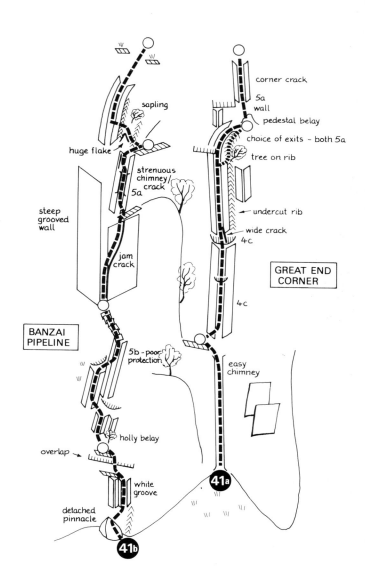

corner crack

5a
wall

pedestal belay

choice of exits - both 5a

tree on rib

undercut rib

wide crack
4c

4c

GREAT END CORNER

sapling

huge flake

strenuous chimney/crack
5a

steep grooved wall

jam crack

BANZAI PIPELINE

5b - poor protection

easy chimney

holly belay

overlap

white groove

detached pinnacle

41a

41b

42: (a) Praying Mantis (HVS+) 85m
(b) DDT (HVS+) 75m

Summary: Two long hard climbs. The rock is mainly good though there are some doubtful bits. Abseil descent.

First Ascent: Praying Mantis – Les Brown and Steve Bradshaw, May 1965. DDT – Jim Lee, Alan Jackman and Paul Ross, October 1965 (with four aid points; climbed free by Ado Liddell).

Best Conditions: North facing at 300m. Allow two good drying days after heavy summer rain.

Approach: Turn west off the B5289, Keswick – Borrowdale road, about 1.5km (1 mile) south of the Borrowdale Hotel, where a picturesque bridge leads to Grange. Turn south in the village on to a rough track. This leads to Hollows Farm Campsite and a small clearing where a few cars can be parked. From an ugly toilet block nearby, a path leads over a stile and up to the crag GR:245 165. 15mins.

Starting Point: Go up a wide quartzy ramp to the right. From its top an undercut buttress is seen up on the right, with a huge bulging wall to its right again (Footless Crow, E5). Hidden in the corner at the junction of the under-cut buttress and this wall is a V-groove that forms the first pitch of Praying Mantis. DDT starts on the left-hand side of the undercut buttress, on a little grass ledge at the foot of a right-angle groove.

Descent: Best made by making several abseils from trees to the left of DDT. The alternative is a very long detour up and then left.

Goat Crag has some good route names – The Blaspheming Butterfly, The Cursing Caterpillar, Praying Mantis, and DDT which takes a knock-out line through the lot. It was Praying Mantis that started the ball rolling – yet another Les Brown *fait accompli*. Inclusion in a certain picture book ensures a reverently worn path to its foot, though the compulsory 5b jamming on the first pitch soon sorts out them what haven't had a good gritstone upbringing! Puzzled, these poor souls often head off round the corner for a bash at DDT, only to retreat with egos further swatted after finding not a single runner on the first ten metres.

But once the initial grunting is over, Praying Mantis opens up and allows enjoyment of the complex route-finding and beautifully positioned problems on its exposed walls and slabs. Protection is always reasonable, unlike that on DDT where some ingenuity is required to find secure runners. The climbing on DDT is steep, difficult and without rests, until the upper corner has been gained, where it eases off a little. It is a great mistake to think of either climb as 'mere' Hard VS.

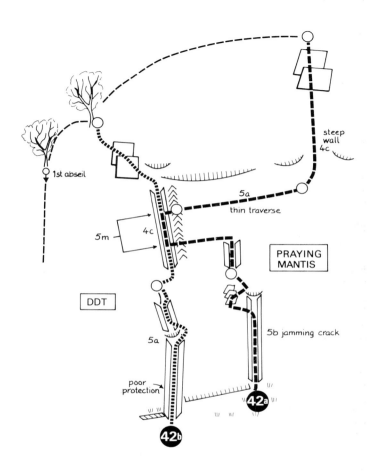

1st abseil

steep wall 4c

5a thin traverse

5m 4c

PRAYING MANTIS

DDT

5b jamming crack

5a

poor protection

42a

42b

43: BLEAK HOWE

(a) Bleak Howe Buttress (E1) 30m
(b) The Reiver (HVS) 30m
(c) Fancy Free (HVS) 30m
(d) Brush Off (HVS) 30m

Summary: A series of highly enjoyable one-pitch climbs on a delightful buttress of recent discovery. Can be combined with routes on Eagle Crag (Route 44).

First Ascent: Bleak Howe Buttress – Dave Hellier, November 1983. Fancy Free and Brush Off – Colin Downer, Sue Kysow and Chris Bacon, May 1984. The Reiver – Downer, June 1984.

Best Conditions: Although it faces north-west at 200m, the crag is well placed to catch the breeze and will recover quickly from showers. Allow two days for heavier rain, longer in winter or spring.

Approach: 10km (6 miles) south of Keswick on the B5289 Borrowdale road, take a turn-off east to Stonethwaite (where there is a small car-park). Follow a bridle path through Stonethwaite Farm Campsite to a footbridge. Cross this and the crag faces you a short distance up the hillside ahead. It is best to head up to the bottom left of the crag and follow a path under its foot to a large boulder – a good picnic platform. GR:273 124. 20mins.

Starting Point: The crag consists of slabs on the left with a fine curving arête to their right (directly above the picnic platform). To the right of the arête is a bay and to the right again the main buttress. Bleak Howe Buttress and The Reiver start at the lowest point of the main buttress below a small slab. Fancy Free starts at the right hand side of the curving arête and Brush Off below the slabs some 5m to the left of Fancy Free.

Descent: To either side of the crag or by abseil. All require care.

These Bleak Howe routes became instant hits amongst the Lakeland locals almost before the dust had settled from Downer's prolific wire brush. Though only a few years old, they have all received many ascents.

The technical crux of Bleak Howe Buttress is a thin move across the first slab, but the real crunch comes above, where a steep groove peters out half way up an impending wall. The cautious will flick a sling over the jug on the left before committing themselves to the reach – and to the strenuous swing and foot scrabbling mantelshelf that follow. Beyond lies a welcome return to slabby rock and an easier finish.

The other routes described are all highly enjoyable: the lines are obvious, the rock good, and protection reasonable where it matters.

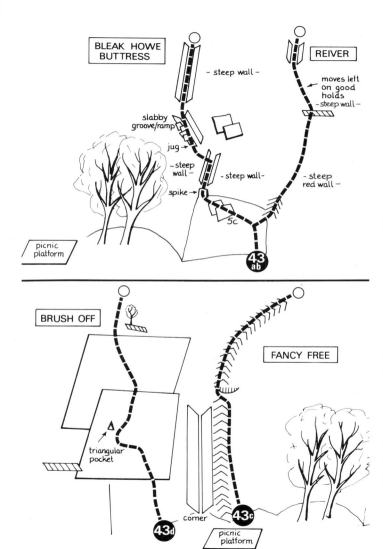

BLEAK HOWE BUTTRESS

REIVER

- steep wall -

moves left on good holds
- steep wall -

slabby groove/ramp

jug

- steep wall -
- steep wall -

- steep red wall -

spike

5c

43 ab

BRUSH OFF

FANCY FREE

triangular pocket

corner

43c

picnic platform

43d

picnic platform

44: (a) Where Eagles Squawk (E2) 60m
(b) Falconer's Crack (VS) 65m

Summary: Drastic surgery and a silly name have brought one of the best hard routes in the valley within the scope of this book. The true lines are indicated on the diagram for the benefit of purists and unconvinceables. Falconer's Crack has some strenuous moments, and is not always well protected. Combine with Route 43 for a full day.

First Ascent: Falconer's Crack – Bill Peascod and Bert Beck, June 1946. Squawk – Brian Henderson and Ken Moseley, June 1965 (with aid; freed by Pete Botterill and Steve Clegg, August 1978). Where Eagles Dare – Pete Whillance and Steve Clegg, August 1975.

Best Conditions: North-east facing at 450m. The crag is slow to ˚ry and extremely slimy when wet. Allow at least three dry summer days for comfort (longer earlier in the season).

Approach: As for Bleak Howe Buttress (refer to Route 43) as far

as Stonethwaite. Then either continue as for Bleak Howe, finally skirting round to the left and up to the crag, or, from the village, cross Stonethwaite Beck via a footbridge and follow a path south-east along the far bank until another bridge allows a return crossing. Eagle Crag dominates the left-hand skyline of the hill ahead and is reached over several boggy fields. GR:277 122. 30mins.

Starting Point: From the grassy scree amphitheatre at the bottom left of the crag, sramble up an exposed rightwards-slanting groove to grass ledges below the crag. Two short ramps slanting left and right form a V at this point. Where Eagles Squawk begins below the left-hand of twin grooves, at a large embedded flake, at the top of the left-hand ramp. Falconer's Crack starts up a hidden off-width left of a low roof, some way up the right-hand ramp.

Descent: To the left of the crag down a grotty open gully.

Dubious cannibalism notwithstanding, the connection of Squawk and Where Eagles Dare results in as nicely a balanced brace of sustained pitches as one is likely to find anywhere. The crux comes high on the second – just when biceps are bulging. A peg is there, thank goodness, though it shows its years. A strenuous rest is possible here but probably unwise when one thin move is all that stands between you and the final arête – a shared finish with Falconer's Crack.

    All the difficult features of Falconer's, of which there are several, succumb best to a bold approach. A handy euphemism this for what is generally taken to imply little gear and much fright.

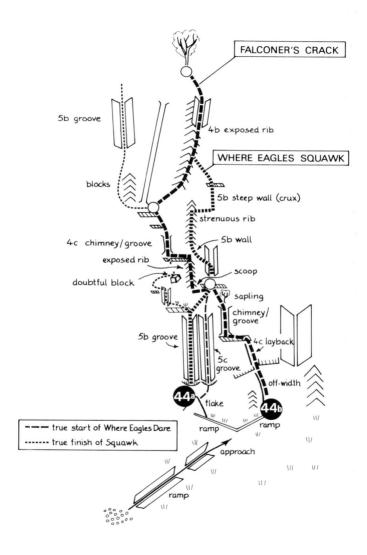

FALCONER'S CRACK

5b groove

4b exposed rib

WHERE EAGLES SQUAWK

blocks

5b steep wall (crux)

strenuous rib

4c chimney/groove

5b wall

exposed rib

scoop

doubtful block

sapling

chimney/groove

5b groove

4c layback

5c groove

off-width

44a

flake

44b

ramp

ramp

— — — true start of Where Eagles Dare
· · · · · true finish of Squawk

approach

ramp

45: SERGEANT CRAG GULLY (S or II/III) 120m

Summary: A good gully, climbable in any conditions if one doesn't mind getting a little damp. A difficult crux and some doubtful rock on the upper pitches.

First Ascent: Owen Glynne Jones, John Robinson, September 1893.

Best Conditions: North-west facing at 400m. In summer the gully is more entertaining if there is plenty of water pouring down it. Being low-lying, it needs a good cold spell to freeze. If there is ice on Derwentwater then it should be in good condition.

Approach: 10km (6 miles) south of Keswick on the B5289, Borrow-dale road, take a turn-off east to Stonethwaite (where there is a small car-park). Follow a bridle path through Stonethwaite Farm Campsite. After crossing a foot-bridge continue along the path that runs south-west on the east bank of Langstrath Beck for about 1km (½ mile). A short stomp up the hillside reaches the gully which cuts up through the left side of the crag (GR:274 114). 30mins.

Starting Point: At the foot of the gully, or avoid the first pitch by grass on the left.

Descent: By a long detour up and left to avoid the crag.

In winter, the difficulties encountered in Sergeant Crag Gully are entirely dependent on the depth of snow and length of freeze. Pick the right day and it's as good as done.

In summer it's a different game altogether; shattered rock, dead sheep, and icy water that delights in streaming into upturned sleeves at every opportunity. In fact you've got to be keen as mustard and just a little bit mad to enjoy it all. But when the weather is low, and spirits likewise, it can prove a lot more entertaining than attempting to find a free handhold on the Ambleside climbing wall.

From too much love of living,
    From ice and snow set free,
We clasp with brief thanksgiving,
    Whatever Thanks may be,
That leaders fall off never,
    And even in the roughest weather,
The weariest climber ever,
    Winds somewhere safe to tea.

From the visitor's book at Seathwaite, quoted in the
Fell & Rock Journal (1923).

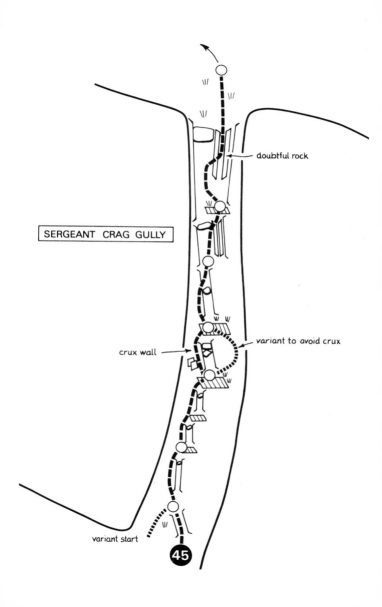

SERGEANT CRAG GULLY

doubtful rock

crux wall

variant to avoid crux

variant start

45

46: RAVEN CRAG GULLY (VD or III/IV) 160m

07/07/07 Ash, Phil

Summary: One of the best winter gully climbs in the Lakes – when in condition. Not such a brilliant summer route, but still worthwhile.

First Ascent: William Wilson and John Wilson Robinson, September 1893. Direct finish added by Owen Glynne Jones, C.W. Patchell and Herbert Bowen, April 1897.

Best Conditions: North-west facing at 400m. Being low-lying, it needs a good cold spell to freeze. If there is ice on Derwentwater then it should be in good condition. In summer the last pitch resembles a bed of vertical sea-weed; for its ascent one either requires a drought, or, like the first ascensionists, nailed boots. It is debatable which is easier to find these days.

Approach: The nearest official parking is at Seatoller on the B5289, Keswick–Borrowdale road. From the car park, walk back towards Keswick for about 500m, and cross a hump-back bridge by some cottages. Turn right and go down a farm lane for a short way (limited parking space on the right, a little further on) and then go left over a stile and follow a track up into Combe Ghyll. The crag is situated on the right at the head of the combe. GR:248 114. 1hr.

Starting Point: Raven Crag Gully is the very deep gully that splits the crag to the right of centre. Start at its foot.

Descent: Turn left and cross a broken stone wall at the top of the buttress. Follow a path behind this down to the left of the crag.

Raven Crag Gully is a natural watercourse, and after a prolonged cold period the build-up of ice is stunningly picturesque – particularly on the final pitch where great swathes of the frozen grail cascade in solid motion over perfectly angled slabs. Below lie steep grooves and a testing cave; above, a single overhanging chockstone. Splendid country for front-pointing technique. This, plus the relatively gentle walk-in, ensures that there is no shortage of cagouled and Koflached figures jangling a path to its foot (when conditions are right).

As a climb it is somewhat reminiscent of an alpine route – as the day warms up, the lower pitches have a worrying tendency to disintegrate without warning. But such is the appeal of Raven Crag Gully that even those arriving at the crag at an unpleasantly alpine hour may often find themselves in a typical Chamonix scrimmage.

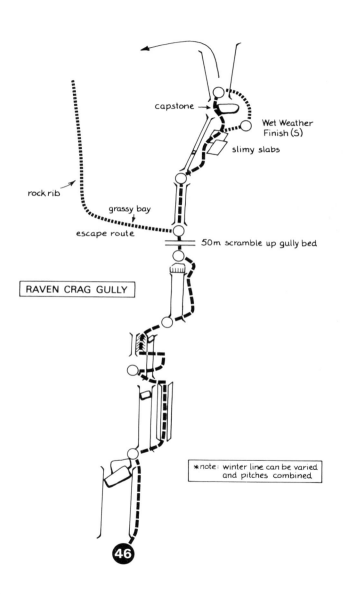

capstone

Wet Weather
Finish (S)

slimy slabs

rock rib

grassy bay

escape route

50m scramble up gully bed

RAVEN CRAG GULLY

*note: winter line can be varied
and pitches combined

46

47: CORVUS (D) 170m

Summary: A masterpiece. Long and sustained with firm rock and good stances. Eminently suitable for beginners.

First Ascent: Bentley Beetham, June 1950.

Best Conditions: North-east facing at 400m and rather vegetated, and so dries slowly. However the rock is clean and it can be climbed under most conditions.

Approach: As for Raven Crag Gully (refer to Route 46).

Starting Point: To the left of Raven Crag Gully is the much shallower Tyro's Gully. Start directly left of this at some well-worn slabs (this is just right of the lowest point of the crag).

Descent: Cross a broken stone wall at the top of the buttress and follow a path behind this down to the left of the crag.

If you climb regularly in Borrowdale, you will almost certainly have been up at least one of Bentley Beetham's routes. Beetham was a schoolmaster from Barnard Castle and required suitable introductory rock for his pupils, whom he brought to stay in the school's club hut in Rosthwaite. Finding the traditional beginner's climbs ridiculously overcrowded, he set out to establish his own. Often climbing solo, as in the case of Corvus, he was responsible for nearly every new route climbed in the area over a thirty year period.

Raven Crag is huge, but its dripping walls and hanging-gardens would seem to defy any attempt at finding a logical line of ascent apart from the gullies. Yet Corvus is just that, and is all the more enjoyable for its devious nature. Cunning but natural sidesteps weave groove, rib and wall into a glorious unity, culminating in the infamous Hand Traverse. Despite the best series of holds you could hope to find, the tension mounts until a hidden stance is won and with it the key to the top.

The wonder of Corvus is that such a long route should be so brilliantly sustained at its grade. It is extraordinary that it should have been so long in the discovering.

'There are too few Mustagh Towers, Drus, Matterhorns and Napes Needles, and so we have to increase the interest in attaining the summit by setting the course where difficulty lies; but once the route has been decided upon we must follow it scrupulously, or regard our effort to do the climb as a failure.' Bentley Beetham, *F&RCC Borrowdale Guide* (1953).

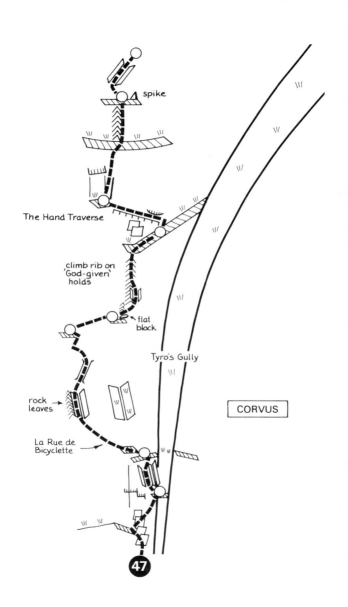

spike

The Hand Traverse

climb rib on
'God-given'
holds

flat
block

Tyro's Gully

rock
leaves

CORVUS

La Rue de
Bicyclette

47

48: (a) Central Gully (II) 320m
(b) South-East Gully (II/III) 220m

Summary: Good, long, winter gully climbs. Protection is usually reasonable (a deadman is handy). Central Gully has several finishes of different grades.

First Ascent: Uncertain in winter. Haskett Smith climbed them both in the autumn of 1882.

Best Conditions: North-west facing at 800m. Great End comes into condition earlier, and stays in condition longer, than anywhere else in the Lakes, with the possible exception of the Helvellyn Corries. Central Gully is prone to avalanche.

Approach: 1 From Seathwaite in Borrowdale. Follow the Styhead track south as far as a small hump-backed bridge (Stockley Bridge).

Cross this and turn left (south) to follow Grains Gill to the crag. GR:236 122 – not to be confused with Great End Crag. 2hrs.
2 From Wasdale Head. Take the Styhead track to Styhead Pass, then follow a path east and then south-east, skirting Sprinkling Tarn to the south to reach the crag. 2hrs 15mins.

Starting Point: Central Gully is unmistakable – a huge right-slanting rift, just right of centre of the crag. South-East Gully is the prominent gully to the left of Central.

Descent: To the left of the crag, or possibly by descending Cust's Gully (bridged chockstone) towards the right of the crag.

Nothing in life is certain, so it is said, except death and income tax. And least certain of all is reliable ice in the foggy monsoon that usually passes for a typical Lakeland winter (remarkably similar to a typical Lakeland summer, as it happens). *But* if there's the slightest hint of frost in the air then Great End is the place to go looking.

Here you will find two excellent gullies, one of which has so many variation finishes it is like having three or four routes in one. There are also other things to consider: Cust's, with its impressive rock scenery, is a good beginner's route (but don't be perturbed by people descending past you); Window, another multi-variation climb, can be very good (if distinctly lacking in protection); while the two grooves to the left of South-East probably come into condition more often than is generally realised (the left-hand one is particularly exciting). Moreover, buttress climbs can be made almost anywhere to the right of Central; and of course, for lateral thinkers, there is always the Great End Girdle.

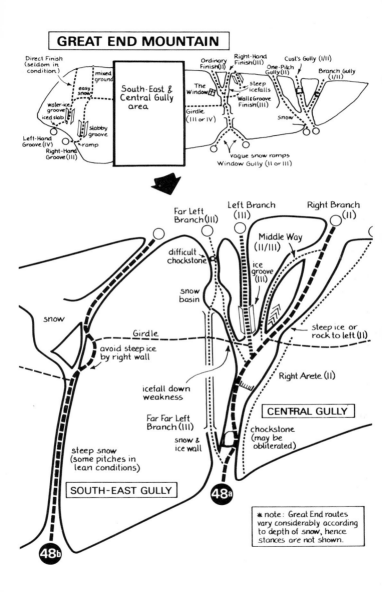

49: GILLERCOMBE BUTTRESS (S–) 330m

Summary: Very good climbing, though whilst heather may be lucky it does spoil the route a little. Some individual moves are hard for the grade but the protection is good at these points.

First Ascent: Harry Lyon and W. Arthur Woodsend, May 1912 (modern finish added by Jack Ray, Henry 'Bones' Harland, Godfrey Solly and Graham Wilson, May 1921).

Best Conditions: South-east facing at 500m. Quick drying, but slimy when wet.

Approach: Easiest on the feet via Honister Pass Youth Hostel (GR:225 135). From the car-park, take a diagonally leftward line up a grassy shoulder to the south. The crag can be seen from the top of the shoulder and is reached quickly by contouring to the right. GR:223 124. Note: marked 'Raven Crag' on some maps. 20mins. The crag can also be approached from Seathwaite (GR:236 122) via Sourmilk Ghyll (located due west) and a bog. 1 hr.

Starting Point: A path traverses under the main bulk of the crag to a fence and stile, directly in line with a small lower buttress below. Cross the stile and continue left for 10m or so to some slabs on the immediate right of a prominent grassy gully.

Descent: It is best to descend the second major gully (it is straight, wide and full of scree) encountered when traversing left along the cliff top. Do not be tempted to leave it for grassy ledges on the left, two-thirds of the way down.

Gillercombe or Grey Knotts Crag was a chance discovery arising out of a short-cut back from Pillar. At the time the only routes in Borrowdale, despite what Lyon termed 'the happy crowd of enthusiasts who arrive with unfailing regularity each Whitsuntide' were a handful of gullies. He resolved forthwith to make a route on his new crag, but then forgot about the place for several years until he finally returned – on a Whit meet.

The best climbing on the route is found in the first few pitches, culminating in an exciting diagonal traverse across an overhanging wall. A wafer-like flake here proved too fine for threading thick hemp rope, and on later ascents Lyon took a large nail for use as a primitive piton. Easier climbing beyond this section is unfortunately broken by two extensive terraces, but these are soon forgotten in the tremendous climbing of the 'modern' finish with its difficult start and screaming exposure. As Lyon later wrote, 'To any frequenter of Borrowdale who, like the Athenians of old, begins to yearn for some new thing, I can recommend a day on Gillercombe Buttress.'

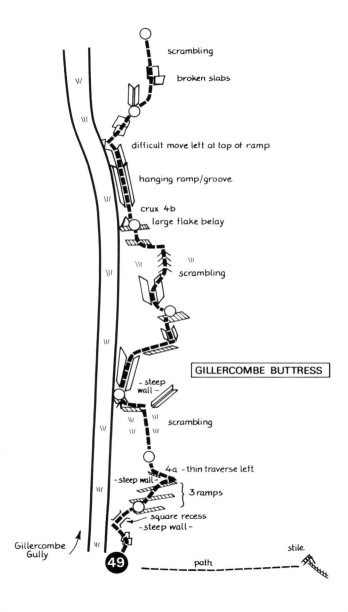

scrambling

broken slabs

difficult move left at top of ramp

hanging ramp/groove

crux 4b

large flake belay

scrambling

GILLERCOMBE BUTTRESS

- steep
wall -

scrambling

4a - thin traverse left

- steep wall -

3 ramps

square recess

- steep wall -

Gillercombe
Gully

49

path

stile

Eastern Fells

Eastern Fells is a convenient label for a vast and diverse area containing relatively few crags of importance, most of which have little in common. A mountain cliff such as Scrubby may possess only one route that merits the accolade 'classic', whilst the roadside gymnasium of Castle Rock is seamed with good lines (reticence has proved essential to maintain a balance). Others like Raven and Dove are famed for ultra-hard climbs, many of which are beyond the scope of this book; yet on both crags are routes where the more modest climber can experience the thrill of extreme territory. Relatively unknown on the eastern extremity are the small but sparkling climbs of Gouther whilst at an opposite compass the Crack of Deer Bield suffers undeserved infamy. Minor crags like these have little room for absorbing crowds and, whilst they will often be empty, it is worth making sure of your route by going at other than peak times.

   The Eastern Fells provide some of the most reliable winter climbing in the Lakes. Four routes are described and others indicated.

Approaches: The western section is well served by the A591 Windermere to Keswick road. Most of the other crags are best reached from the A592 Windermere to Penrith road, which reaches Patterdale via the Kirkstone Pass (notorious for becoming snowbound). Swindale is reached from Shap, on the A6 Kendal to Penrith road. All these major towns are linked by bus. Railway stations at Kendal, Windermere and Penrith.

Acommodation: *Camping*: High Bridgend Farm (GR:315 194) and Dale Bottom (GR:296 218) in Thirlmere. Sykeside, near the Brothers Water Inn, (GR:403 119). Gillside, Glenridding (GR:380 168) in Patterdale.
High camps/bivouacs: Possible at all the isolated crags. There is a particularly good hidden cave at Dove Crag.
Youth Hostels: Stanah (GR:319 190) at Thirlmere, Butharlyp How (GR:336 076) and Thorny How (GR:332 084) at Grasmere, Goldrill House (GR:399 157) at Patterdale, and Greenside (GR:366 174) at Glenridding.
Hotels: Guest houses and hotels in Glenridding, Patterdale, Grasmere, Ambleside and Keswick. More isolated hotels at Thirlspot and Threlkeld in Thirlmere, Brother's Water, Low Hartsop, and Kirkstone Pass, Patterdale.

Services: Most hotels serve food; cafes and grocers in Glenridding and Patterdale. Climbing shops in Ambleside, Kendal, Keswick, Penrith and Windermere. Petrol at Ullswater, Ambleside and Keswick. 24 hour petrol is at Canal Garage, Crooklands (on the A65 where it passes under the M6 north of Junction 36) and at Penrith.

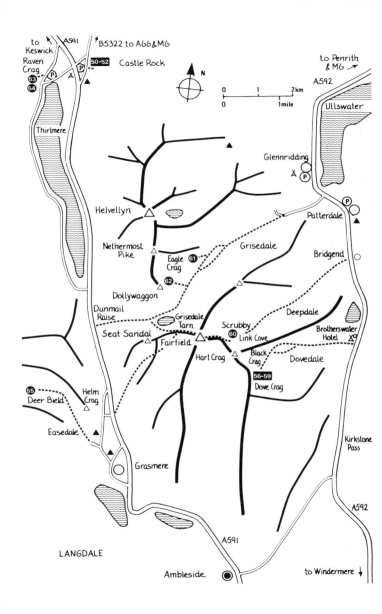

50: NORTH CRAG ELIMINATE (E1) 80m

Summary: A route of distinction that, more than most, requires techniques from our primal past. Protection is reasonable but worryingly distant from the difficult moves.

First Ascent: Harold Drasdo and Dennis Gray, September 1952.

Best Conditions: North facing at 250m. The crag is slow to dry once thoroughly wet, but its low lying position' and overhanging nature helps it to recover quickly from showers.

Approach: From the A591 Ambleside to Keswick road, turn north on the B5322 towards St John's-in-the-Vale. The crag is clearly visible on the right. There is a large car park on the left, just beyond the Youth Hostel. Cross over the road into the field below the crag (stile). A stile and foot-bridge over an aqueduct at the top left-hand corner of the field provide access. (GR: 322 197). 10mins.

Starting Point: Immediately to the left of the wall that runs up to the foot of the crag.

Descent: Either descend a greasy and rather loose gully (M) to the left, or make a long detour to the right around South Crag.

The earliest serious explorations at Castle Rock were those of Graham Macphee, who made numerous visits during the notoriously wet summer of 1928. Attempts on the 'above plumb' North Face were foiled by a combination of meteorology, geology and forestry (wet, loose, vegetated rock). Macphee cannily prophesied that 'volumes might be written about the botany of the crag; but not by me. The cautious climber may even go off route to attain arboreal excrescences. . .'

  North Crag Eliminate is a climb of such charm that it was guaranteed to become popular. Inevitably, the upper branches of the stout yew on the penultimate pitch have suffered: to such an extent that a longer reach than that made by the two 'Bradford Lads' is now needed to gain good holds. The final pitch is simply superb: a slender, overhung ramp that narrows and forces a blind swing. Protection is available, but you will feel as much out on a limb as on the tree pitch. Beyond the arête lurks a shallow and unfriendly groove, though, as Drasdo said at the time, 'It's only vertical round there.'

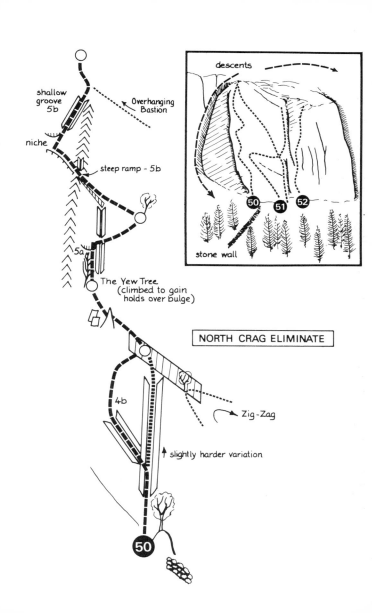

shallow
groove
5b

niche

Overhanging
Bastion

steep ramp - 5b

5a

The Yew Tree
(climbed to gain
holds over bulge)

NORTH CRAG ELIMINATE

4b

Zig-Zag

↑ slightly harder variation

descents

50   51   52

stone wall

50

51: (a) Overhanging Bastion (VS) 85m
(b) Zig-Zag (VS) 110m

Summary: Excellent, classic climbs in impressive surroundings. Very useful for an evening visit, when they catch the sun.

First Ascent: Both routes – Jim Birkett, Charlie Wilson and Len Muscroft, April 1939.

Best Conditions: North facing at 250m. The crag is slow to dry once thoroughly wet, but its low lying position and overhanging nature helps it to recover quickly from showers.

Approach: Refer to Route 50.

Starting Point: Zig-Zag – 10m right of the stone wall at a small pinnacle. Overhanging Bastion – 10m right again, beneath a gnarled holly. (Refer also to Route 50 inset diagram.)

Descent: Either descend a greasy and rather loose gully (M) to the left, or make a long detour to the right around South Crag.

The North Face of Castle Rock is one of the most approachable and impressive rock walls in the Lakes, which makes it all the more curious that no one had triumphed over the challenge of its great slanting central line prior to 1939. The answer is quite simple: no one dared.

Overhanging Bastion, an extraordinary route, required an extraordinary man to lead it – Jim Birkett. Those were still the days of the gentleman climber, yet he was a quarry worker who had left school at fourteen. Toughened by his job, and with an intimate knowledge of the fells, he came to dominate Lakeland climbing for a decade, putting up difficult new routes of high quality in almost every area. Overhanging Bastion was one of his earliest, and made a great impression on the climbing scene. (Likewise the press, who unfortunately hailed it as the 'Lakeland Everest Conquered'.)

Unusually for Birkett, who did most of his routes in nails, he climbed in rubbers that April Fool's Day. One sling was all the protection he found on the ramp, and even this fell off as he calmly removed handfuls of loose rock from the steep little wall near its top, before moving up on the remaining ricketty tusks. He rated his breakthrough as easy for Very Severe. Perhaps it is – except for a devil of a move off the pinnacle on the main pitch, and for the incredible exposure throughout.

Zig-Zag was put up by the same team three weeks later. Whilst not as important as Overhanging Bastion, it is still an excellent climb and, being easier, makes a good introduction to the crag.

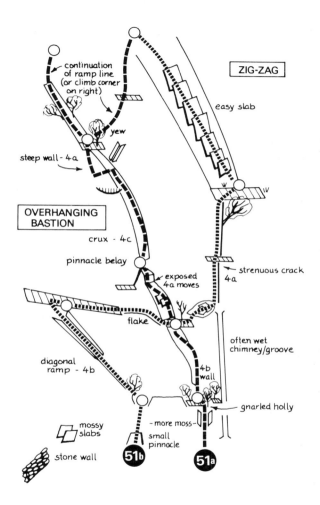

ZIG-ZAG

continuation
of ramp line
(or climb corner
on right)

easy slab

yew

steep wall - 4a

OVERHANGING
BASTION

crux - 4c

pinnacle belay

exposed
4a moves

strenuous crack
4a

flake

often wet
chimney/groove

diagonal
ramp - 4b

4b
wall

gnarled holly

mossy
slabs

- more moss -
small
pinnacle

stone wall

51b

51a

52: THIRLMERE ELIMINATE (E1) 55m

Summary: A climb of contrasts: irritatingly awkward on the first pitch, very bold on the second. Strenuous, technical and well protected on the crux.

First Ascent: Paul Ross and Pete Greenwood, June 1955 (with one point of aid; Joe Brown and Don Whillans straightened out the top pitch in 1956).

Best Conditions: North facing at 250m. The crag is slow to dry once thoroughly wet, but its low lying position and overhanging nature helps it to recover quickly from showers. Note that the lower reaches take longer to dry. Allow three dry summer days.

Approach: Refer to Route 50.

Starting Point: A few metres right of the start of Overhanging Bastion (Route 51) is an often-wet chimney/groove line. On the wall 5m to the right of this is a large perched flake. Start below the flake. (Refer also to Route 50 inset diagram.)

Descent: Either descend a greasy and rather loose gully (M) to the left, or make a long detour to the right around South Crag.

Before his untimely death in 1953, Arthur Dolphin had firmly established the new *Extreme* grade. But while the Rock and Ice consolidated their similar advance in Wales, the North had been robbed of the one man who would have matched their efforts in Lakeland. To a certain extent others filled the breach; notably Pete Greenwood, another of the Bradford Lads, who had often partnered Dolphin. Greenwood was a determined character who made a number of notable first ascents in the short span of time before he unexpectedly stopped climbing in 1956. One famous deed was his repeat of Kipling Groove shortly after Joe Brown had placed a peg on the crux. Greenwood merely spat on the offending ironmongery, before completing the pitch to rousing cheers from onlookers below.

Another rapidly rising star was Paul Ross, who was soon to spearhead development in Borrowdale. He had only been climbing a year when he did Thirlmere Eliminate, succeeding on the top pitch after Greenwood had used up all his strength placing a peg over the bulge. Ross later described the crux as being of the 'up or off' variety.

The following year it was to be Ross who, with his lead of Post Mortem on Eagle Crag, Borrowdale, would establish the 5c grade in the Lakes for the first time – a welcome riposte to the Welsh challenge.

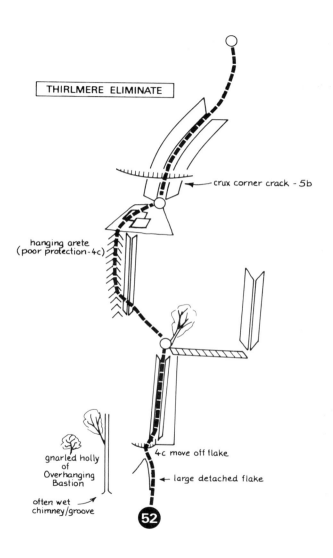

THIRLMERE ELIMINATE

crux corner crack – 5b

hanging arete
(poor protection – 4c)

gnarled holly
of
Overhanging
Bastion

often wet
chimney/groove

4c move off flake

large detached flake

52

53: COMMUNIST CONVERT (VS) 45m

Summary: This highly exposed climb – with much traversing and spartan protection – is not for beginners. Technical difficulty is low, however, and it is very enjoyable for the competent.

First Ascent: Arthur Dolphin, Don Hopkin, Mike Dwyer and John Ramsden, May 1953.

Best Conditions: East facing at 300m. Although it catches the breeze the crux groove takes several weeks of reasonably good weather to dry out after winter. Allow two dry days in summer.

Approach: The crag lies at the northern end of Thirlmere and is approached initially along the A591 Ambleside to Keswick road. Just north of its junction with the B5322 (St John's Vale) road, a lane leads west over the top of the Thirlmere Dam. Follow the lane to a junction with another minor road. Either park here or turn right and park on the right in 50m. From opposite the second car-park follow a steep foot-path through woods on to a forestry track. Follow the track left to daylight and the crag. GR:304 188. 15mins.

Starting Point: On a large grassy terrace under the huge cave left of centre of the crag (gain the terrace by scrambling up a short hidden chimney at its left-hand end). Start at the foot of a broken slab to the right of the cave.

Descent: Follow the path rightwards from the finishing ledge.

Arthur Rhodes Dolphin was only twenty-eight years old when he died after slipping from an easy descent path in the Mont Blanc range. He had just made the first British ascent of a hard route on the Dent du Geant, and was hoping to prove himself for a mooted second 1953 Everest expedition.

Communist Convert sadly marked the close of a stream of brilliant and daring first ascents by Dolphin that began at Almscliffe in his teenage years with the likes of Demon Wall and Overhanging Groove. While not as technical as many of his other Lakeland climbs, or even those earlier gritstone ones, it was the first real breach of the central area of the formidable Raven Crag. Dolphin's love of puns gave him the name – the route starts on the left but moves to the right.

It begins innocuously enough with a short slab pitch on hollow holds, but with the rightward step to the stance the true nature of the climb is revealed. An old peg shows the way and the rest unfolds like magic – an airy but natural path of the most extreme exposure imaginable.

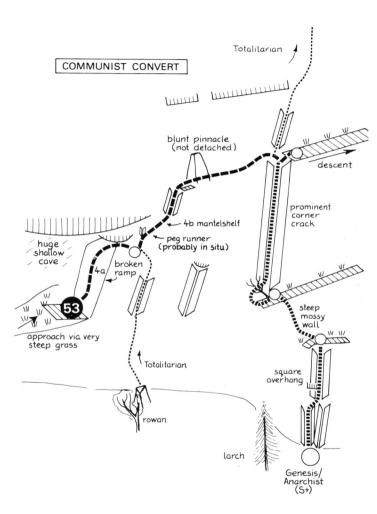

COMMUNIST CONVERT

Totalitarian

descent

blunt pinnacle
(not detached)

4b mantelshelf

peg runner
(probably in situ)

prominent
corner
crack

huge
shallow
cave

4a

broken
ramp

53

steep
mossy
wall

approach via very
steep grass

Totalitarian

square
overhang

rowan

larch

Genesis/
Anarchist
(S+)

54: TOTALITARIAN (E1) 90m

Summary: A powerful route with continually interesting climbing, culminating in a wild finale on the exposed headwall. The first pitch is bold and strenuous, the second sustained and delicate. A point of aid on the slab of the top pitch reduces the technical grade to 5b.

First Ascent: Chris Bonington and Mike Thompson, using one point of aid, September 1964 (climbed free by Ed Grindley).

Best Conditions: East facing at 300m. Although it catches the breeze the groove on the third pitch takes several weeks of reasonably good weather to dry out after winter. Allow two dry days in summer. Beware – the midges on this crag hunt in packs.

Approach: Refer to Route 53.

Starting Point: Underneath the steep central wall grows an isolated rowan. Behind this a huge detached block forms the first belay.

Descent: By a path to the right.

Chris Bonington is the best known of British mountaineers. His achievements are formidable: first ascents on rock and ice throughout the British Isles and the Alps; first British ascent of the North Face of the Eiger; leader of numerous successful expeditions to the Himalayas; Everest at 50; and a stream of eminently readable books that appeal to layman and expert alike. Totalitarian slots into the middle of all this – somewhere between Patagonia and Annapurna – a gleaming gem overshadowed by the greater ranges.

Four contrasting pitches, including the best section of Communist Convert, conspire to present a magnificent challenge with a daunting finale. A peg, once used for aid, now protects the steep slab under the final overhangs. Here all the intensity of 5c difficulty is condensed into one long flick of the right foot, as fingers struggle with miniscule holds before grasping high for a superb slot. A swing out right on to the headwall evades the eaves to attain a superbly exposed jamming crack. At its top throw caution to the wind and make a series of wild layaways on the ebb of strength for a truly stunning finish to one of Lakeland's greatest hard climbs.

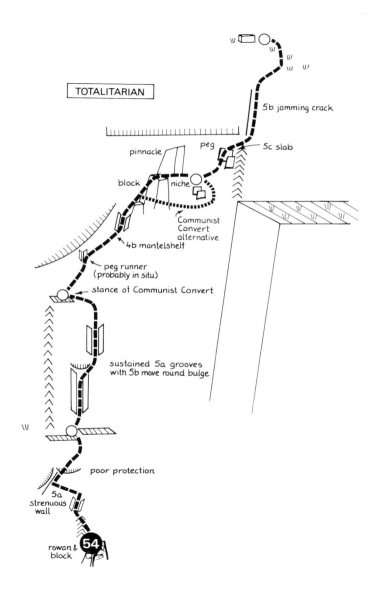

TOTALITARIAN

5b jamming crack

peg

5c slab

pinnacle

block

niche

Communist
Convert
alternative

4b mantelshelf

peg runner
(probably in situ)

stance of Communist Convert

sustained 5a grooves
with 5b move round bulge

poor protection

5a
strenuous
wall

rowan &
block

54

55: (a) Deer Bield Crack (HVS) 60m
(b) Deer Bield Buttress (E1) 70m

Summary: Two difficult climbs of great historical importance. Sadly, rockfall has recently affected the upper section of the Buttress and the stability of the remaining rock is supect. Take care, particularly after the frost action of a hard winter.

First Ascent: Deer Bield Crack – Albert Thompson Hargeaves and George Graham Macphee, February 1930. Deer Bield Buttress – Arthur Dolphin and A.D Brown, June 1951.

Best Conditions: The crag faces north-east at 400m but takes little drainage; both routes dry very quickly in summer.

Approach: Park in Grasmere village centre and follow an un-classified tarmac road signed to Easedale Tarn that leads north by north-east (do not try to drive up this road – there really is nowhere to park). Now follow signs for Far Easedale until clear of the farms. Follow the path along Far Easedale Gill until Deer Bield Crag suddenly appears halfway up the hillside on the left. GR:303 097. 1hr.

Starting Point: High in the centre of the crag is a wide chimney. This forms the crux of the Crack, which starts directly beneath at an embedded flake. The Buttress starts 3m to the right at a large leftward-slanting slab bounded on its right by bulging walls and a hanging groove.

Descent: To the left.

Like many Lakeland climbers, A.T. Hargeaves began his climbing career on gritstone, producing a number of fine routes, including Black Slab at Stanage. In 1929, after failing on the Buttress, he turned his attention to the Crack. But it was too wet, and it was the following year before he finally succeeded on a top rope after two hours of fruitless struggle. He then led it without protection, a tremendous achievement. Now that tiny wires protect the roof it is certainly a less worrying lead, but it still calls for strong legs and grim determination.

Two decades of further attempts passed before the Buttress fell, inevitably, to Dolphin. This bold lead, protected by just two runners, reaffirmed his position at the top of the Lakeland scene.

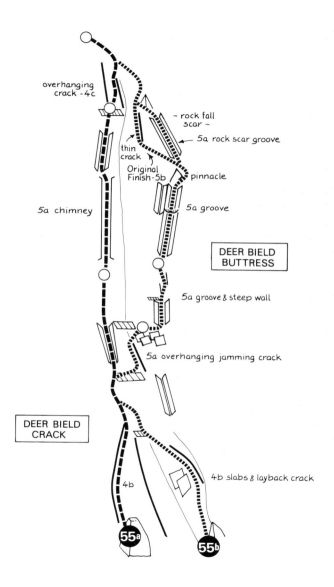

overhanging
crack - 4c

- rock fall
  scar -

5a rock scar groove

thin
crack

Original
Finish - 5b

pinnacle

5a chimney

5a groove

DEER BIELD
BUTTRESS

5a groove & steep wall

5a overhanging jamming crack

DEER BIELD
CRACK

4b

4b slabs & layback crack

55a   55b

56: (a) Inaccessible Gully (IV) 100m
(b) Black Crag Icefall (III/IV) 90m

Summary: Two excellent hard ice climbs situated conveniently close together and thus easily done in a day.

First Ascent: Unknown.

Best Conditions: These crags face north-east; Dove Crag at 750m, and Black Crag at 550m. Both climbs require a prolonged freeze to come into good condition.

Approach: Refer to Route 57. Beyond the intake wall (that is the last wall spanning the valley), the fairly level path curves around to the left before it starts to rise after crossing a stream; the dank mass

of Black Crag stands on the right above this curve. GR:379 116. 50mins. For Inaccessible Gully, initially follow the directions for Route 57, but then head for South Gully which is at the very left end of the crag, to the left of Westmorland's Route (Route 59).

Starting Point: Inaccessible Gully begins 50m up South Gully at the foot of the great icefall that descends from the hanging gully on the right. Black Crag Icefall takes the main fall up the centre of the cliff.

Descent: Inaccessible Gully – refer to Route 59. Black Crag Icefall – to either side of the crag.

These two fine climbs can be found in condition most winters – but not often for very long periods. When they are, their popularity is well evident, to the late riser toiling up the Dovedale path, by the clusters of mobile, multicoloured dots at their respective feet. For Inaccessible this popularity may be welcomed: leading the extremely steep and spectacular first pitch becomes a sight easier once it has been peppered with ice-axe holes. Climbing by numbers. This preconditioning has little effect on the chockstone above, but then in technical terms Inaccessible is really just a one-pitch climb.

In the case of Black Crag Icefall, however, too many heavy-handed axe-men up the crux of the first pitch, where the stream of tumbling ice narrows to body width, can leave hopeful ice-warriors with nothing but curses and an unassailable few feet of bare rock. But if the first pitch has its tricky moments, the second is pure joy – iced slabs, reminiscent of the upper Orion Face in quality (if not in length) – no problem with today's cat's claws. The right-hand finish is also well worthwhile, but be warned – there is little comfort to be gained from either the protection or the belay.

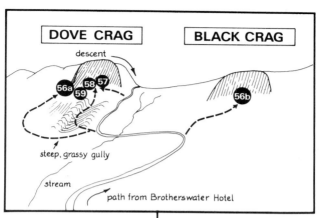

DOVE CRAG

BLACK CRAG

descent

56a 58 57 59

56b

steep, grassy gully

stream

path from Brotherswater Hotel

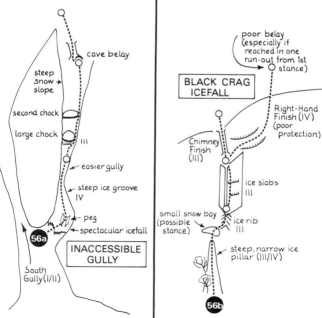

cave belay

steep snow slope

second chock

large chock

III

easier gully

steep ice groove IV

peg

spectacular icefall

56a

South Gully (I/II)

INACCESSIBLE GULLY

poor belay (especially if reached in one run-out from 1st stance)

BLACK CRAG ICEFALL

Right-Hand Finish (IV) (poor protection)

Chimney Finish (III)

ice slabs III

small snow bay (possible stance)

ice rib III

steep, narrow ice pillar (III/IV)

56b

57: EXTOL (E2) 75m

Summary: A long, lonely lead, sustained and strenuous, but not too high in terms of technical difficulty.

First Ascent: Don Whillans and Colin Mortlock, April 1960.

Best Conditions: North-east facing at 750m. Allow at least four or five dry summer days, preferably a week.

Approach: From the Brotherswater Hotel (GR:403 119) on the A592 Ambleside to Penrith road, walk straight through the campsite to Hartsop Hall. Beyond the farm buildings take the right-hand path. Follow this for about an hour, at which point Dove Crag should be a very obvious presence on your left. Refer also to Route 56 diagram. GR:376 109. 1hr.

Starting Point: Traverse left under the cliff face to a central area where a high narrow triangle of easier angled rock is sandwiched between the overhanging walls on either side. The left-hand edge of this triangle forms a chimney that leads to its apex. Scramble through shrubbery to the foot of this chimney.

Descent: Either traverse rightwards along grass, passing a cave, or scramble to the top and descend as for Route 59.

The first pitch of Extol is something of a misfit – a shattered and insecure chimney – wholly out of character with what lies above. Beyond it the rock becomes fantastically steep (though sound, thank heavens), leading to a ferocious, overhanging wall. There is no longer any doubt about what has to be done, but plenty about one's ability to do it. Moreover, a sting in the tail awaits those who injudiciously relax above the overhangs.

Extol has been acknowledged (F&RCC Journal, 1986) as 'probably the most outstanding accomplishment of 1960', itself an exceptional year in the Lakes. The tale is pure Whillans: emerging bruised but victorious from a "dobbing match" the night before. . . wet and greasy rock. . . two and a half hours on the main pitch. . . incessant smoking in extraordinary positions. . . leader and second forced to move together due to excessive run-out. And then there was that telling conversation with a passer-by:

"What route's that?"
"It aint. . . yet."
"Who are you?"
"Whillans."
"Yer must be mad!"

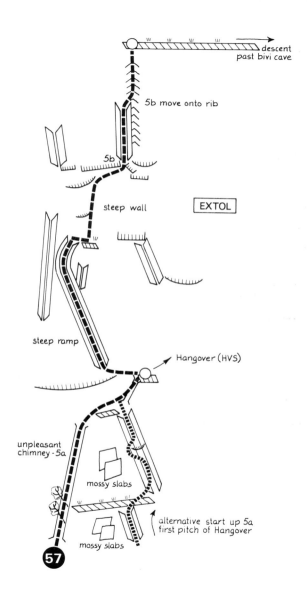

descent
past bivi cave

5b move onto rib

5b

steep wall

EXTOL

steep ramp

Hangover (HVS)

unpleasant
chimney - 5a

mossy slabs

alternative start up 5a
first pitch of Hangover

mossy slabs

57

58: DOVEDALE GROOVE (HVS+) 55m

Summary: A Brown and Whillans groove and crack special. Hard and continuously sustained at its grade.

First Ascent: Don Whillans, Joe Brown and Don Cowan, May 1953 (pitch 4 added by Allan Austin and Jack Soper, June 1963).

Best Conditions: North-east facing at 750m. Allow at least four or five dry summer days.

Approach: Refer to Route 57.

Starting Point: Well to the left of Extol (Route 57), on clean slabs under an impressive, impending groove.

Descent: Refer to Route 59.

Climbing in the early 1950s was dominated by the remarkable partnership of Joe Brown and Don Whillans, the star performers of the newly formed Rock and Ice club. True, they left a far greater mark on the Peak, where they had ruled for years anyway, and Wales, where the lure of Cloggy and the Pass was stronger than anything the Lakes could offer, but nonetheless they visited Cumbria on a number of occasions, repeating Dolphin's routes and leaving us with a few real masterpieces such as Triermain Eliminate on Castle Rock and this, Dovedale Groove, climbed within a few months of each other. Of the two, Dovedale Groove is the easier and more enjoyable proposition. Despite which it soon acquired a formidable reputation as one party after another failed to come to grips with it. A decade passed before it was repeated by another formidable Wales based team consisting of Peter Crew and Baz Ingle.

It is hard to understand now why aid was once required for the first few feet, problematic though they are; a good hold quickly comes to hand and the remainder of the pitch is a delightful, almost elegant series of flowing bridging moves. Real difficulty lies above, where a strenuous off-width must be left awkwardly with the help of a handy jammed flake. For the total purist a mossy wall can be pressed into a third pitch, though it is hard and out of keeping, and is easily avoided on the left. The final rise through the overhangs is quite enough to hold one's interest, and maintain the climb's arm-draining reputation, to the last.

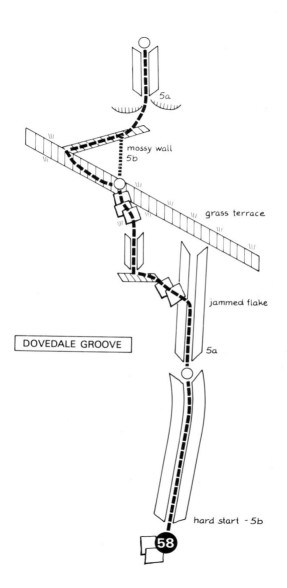

5a

mossy wall
5b

grass terrace

jammed flake

DOVEDALE GROOVE

5a

hard start - 5b

58

59: WESTMORLAND'S ROUTE (VD+) 105m

Summary: A very satisfying mountaineering route despite several paddocks on the upper pitches. Best done with a minimal rack and no other intention than that of continuing on foot to the summit of Fairfield for luncheon.

First Ascent: Horace 'Rusty' Westmorland, John Mounsey and W. Arthur North, October 1910 (the first two pitches were added by Charlie Wilson, Mabel Barker, Douglas Tweddle, Joe Bell and Nan Hamilton in May 1937; they called the route Wing Ridge believing it to be unclimbed).

Best Conditions: North-east facing at 750m. Although Dove Crag requires a prolonged dry spell to bring it into condition, Westmorland's Route should be climbable on most days by a competent party.

Approach: Refer to Route 57.

Starting Point: To the left of Dovedale Groove, at the foot of the sharp ridge which separates the main crag from South Gully. An approach can be made from either side.

Descent: Go straight back from the cliff edge, cross a broken wall and then, trending slightly right but ignoring several tempting gullies on the right, continue back to an easy descent, round to the right of the crag.

Though harder and more open face routes had been climbed elsewhere by 1910, Westmorland's Route (the first on the crag) was the first non-chimney climb to be made in the whole of the Eastern Fells. It was something of a breakthrough as the route has enormous exposure which, together with the lack of any obvious line, lends a sense of uncertainty even to a modern day ascent.

Perhaps the first ascensionists also had their doubts – a local newspaper reported the presence of a physician at the foot of the crags! But Dr Wilkins was there mainly through mountaineering interest, and his professional services were not required. Nevertheless, Westmorland was to recall one heart-stopping moment when he decided the key to the route was a wide, tilted flake leaning against an overhang. There was no belay and as he tentatively climbed the slab it gently slid out with him clinging to it. 'It was nice when after four inches it stopped and I could go on to the little three foot roof-top; stand upon it and with an arm-pull get over the overhang to a ledge.'

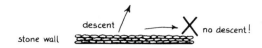

stone wall · descent · no descent!

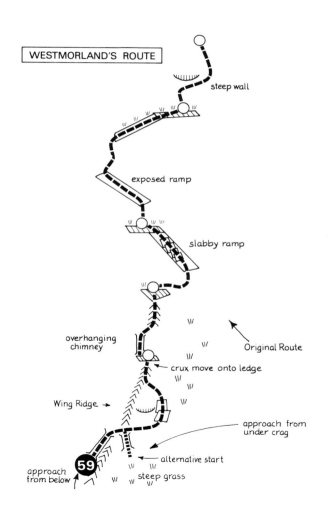

WESTMORLAND'S ROUTE

steep wall

exposed ramp

slabby ramp

overhanging chimney

Original Route

crux move onto ledge

Wing Ridge →

approach from under crag

alternative start

steep grass

approach from below

59

60: GRENDEL (VS) 75m

Summary: An unsung climb of heroic stature and well worth the long walk. In bone dry conditions it only just merits the grade.

First Ascent: Harold Drasdo and Gordon Batty, June 1956.

Best Conditions: South-east facing at 800m. Climbable after two days without rain, but retains wet streaks which make it harder. Allow five dry days for maximum enjoyment.

Approach: 1 Park at Dunmail Raise on the A591 (GR:328 116) and follow Raise Beck to Grisedale Tarn. A path leads around the south-west shore of the tarn to Grisedale Hause (also reached by following Little Tongue Gill from near Grasmere). Head steeply east over the summit of Fairfield and follow the ridge east to the col – Link Hause – between it and Hart Crag. Scrubby Crag is just to the north. GR:367 116. 1hr 15mins.
2 An alternative approach can be made from Patterdale via Deepdale and Link Cove (very boggy), or along the Hartsop above How Ridge which bounds Deepdale to the south. 1hr 45mins.

Starting Point: It is best to leave sacks near Link Hause. Go down scree to a large flake marking the start of a grass terrace which divides the crag from vegetated slabs below. Traverse the terrace to its far right end where a prominent V-groove will be seen. A small spike at the top of the terrace provides the first belay.

Descent: Scramble up left and contour round to Link Hause. The descent from Fairfield can be awkward in bad weather and it is advisable to carry a map and compass.

On Dunmail Raise stands a dark cairn; sandwiched now between two lanes of tourist traffic, it lies forlorn, a distant echo of a long-past age. This grim mound marks the grave of Dunmail, last King of Cumbria. Hurry past in the dim-lit dawn and trudge on up to Grisedale Tarn (here they hurled his golden crown) for Grendel awaits and legends abound.

The first pitch is guarded well, but above initial fumblings turns into the perfect groove, fully equipped with the most magnificent holds. Seconds crane their necks with incredulity as leaders swing courageously from jugs that are invisible from below. Pray that courage does not desert you both, on the smooth, protectionless slab and crumbling overhangs above.

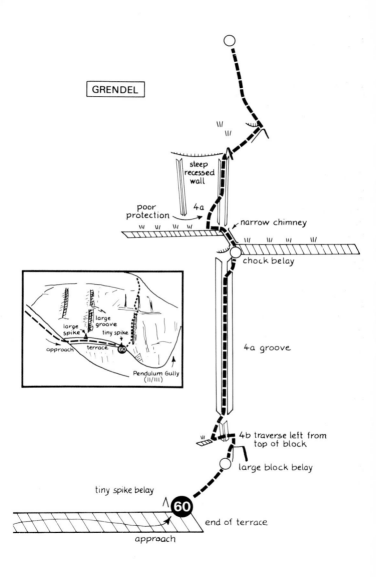

GRENDEL

steep recessed wall

poor protection

4a

narrow chimney

chock belay

4a groove

4b traverse left from top of block

large block belay

tiny spike belay

end of terrace

approach

large spike

large groove

tiny spike

approach

terrace

60

Pendulum Gully (II/III)

61: (a) Kestrel Wall (S) 45m
(b) Sobrenada (VS+) 60m

Summary: An excellent place to visit early in the season. Steep, sunny climbing on first-rate rock. Protection, while not exactly encouraging, is adequate on the harder sections.

First Ascent: Kestrel Wall – Jim Birkett and Harry Griffin, July 1954. Sobrenada – Mike James, George Leaver and K.A. Brookes, June 1957.

Best Conditions: South facing at 400m and dries rapidly. Allow one day after heavy rain.

Approach: 1 From the A592 at Patterdale a road goes south-west into Grisedale (there is no parking whatsoever up this road except within the first fifty metres; if there is no room here then there is a car-park opposite the Patterdale Hotel, 500m to the south). Walk up the road and when it becomes a track, continue along the south bank of Grisedale Beck. Shortly after the last woods, twin crags and some old mine workings will be seen on the opposite side of the river. Cross over to them via a footbridge near a sheepfold. The routes lie on the left-hand crag. GR:357 142. 55mins.

2 An alternative approach can be made from Dunmail Raise on the A591: follow directions as for Route 62 and carry on down into Grisedale to reach the crag. 1hr 15mins.

Starting Point: Both routes lie on the sunny left-hand side of the crag. A slanting ramp runs from left to right across the lower buttress. Sobrenada begins at the base of the slab under this ramp. Kestrel Wall starts at a blunt spike at the foot of the ramp. Two flake grooves split the wall above – Kestrel Wall takes the left-hand one.

Descent: To the left of the crag.

Kestrel Wall was Jim Birkett's last new climb. While not as hard as many of his earlier ones, it is exposed and has two very steep sections – a good farewell from one of the grand masters of Lakeland rock.

Sobrenada is the sort of route that is much easier with a sneaky bit of prior knowledge. The first pitch seems precarious enough, but it is technically a pushover compared to the wall above the Pasture. Initial overhangs are bypassed by a most peculiar leftward step. The position seems anything but VS, and a chimney is reached with misplaced relief. This is where the prior knowledge comes in handy (without it things begin to feel almost *Extreme*). As they've been graded VS you'd better know that the chimney is best chimneyed and that there's a hidden incut at its top. Once this is grasped your worries are almost over.

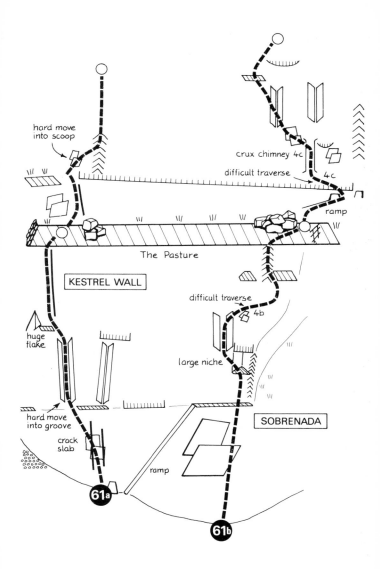

62: (a) Dollywaggon Gully (II/III) 130m
(b) Chock Gully (III/IV) 115m

Summary: Traditional gullies containing traditional chockstones. The upper one in Chock Gully is significantly harder than anything else on the route.

First Ascent: Unknown.

Best Conditions: East facing at 700m. An inland location that holds snow better than elsewhere in the Lakes; often in condition.

Approach: 1 From Dunmail Raise. Refer to Route 60 for the approach to Grisdale Tarn. Now go around the northern shore of the tarn and enter Grisedale. The first major crag to the north is Tarn Crag, and Falcon Crag is its right-ward continuation. GR:351 127. 1hr.

2 From Patterdale. Follow the directions as for Route 60, but carry straight on to the crags which lie above the path at the head of the valley. 1hr 15mins.

Starting Point: Dollywagon Gully is the wide gully starting from the right side of a small amphitheatre on the left of the crag. Chock Gully is the deeply cut gully near the right end of the crag, facing Grisedale.

Descent: Head south by south-west to Grisedale Tarn.

The Helvellyn range is famed for its winter mountaineering and contains many climbs in the lower grades. Dollywaggon and Chock Gullies are two of the best, but others are also worthwhile and can usually be relied on for good sport when the mountains are snow covered. They are described from north to south:

Glenridding: Red Tarn Crag (GR:343 152) – Three distinct gullies on the north-west flank of Helvellyn. The left-hand one is graded III, the others II. The ridges on the left and right are Striding and Swirral Edges respectively (I).

Nethermost Cove: Lad Crag (GR:345 148) – Approach via Grisedale. Four gullies. The best is the right-hand one, starting under Striding Edge. This is Nethermost Gully by the right branch (I/II). The others are II. Large cornices can be a problem.

Ruthwaite Cove: Nethermost Crag (GR:344 139) – The main line is Jogebar Gully (II/III). Several other easy gullies – good icefalls.

In addition there are a number of easy gullies on St Sunday Crag (GR:367 137) and, towards the left side of the crag (look for a high tower with a tree in its left side), the excellent Pinnacle Ridge (I/II, M). On Dove Crag there is South Gully (I/II, refer to Route 56) and at the right-hand side of Scrubby Crag, Pendulum Gully (II/III) is often formed (refer to Route 60).

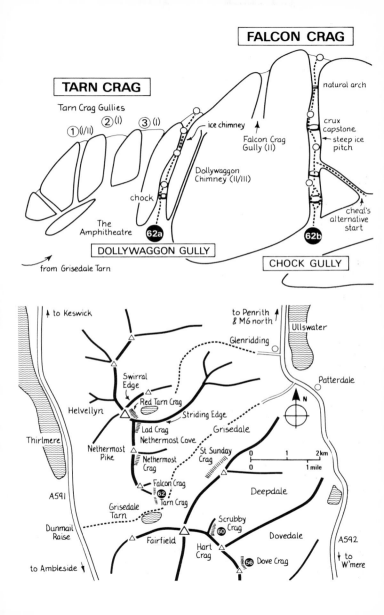

TARN CRAG

Tarn Crag Gullies

① (I/II)   ② (I)   ③ (I)

FALCON CRAG

natural arch

crux capstone

steep ice pitch

ice chimney

Falcon Crag Gully (II)

Dollywaggon Chimney (II/III)

chock

The Amphitheatre

cheat's alternative start

62a

62b

DOLLYWAGGON GULLY

CHOCK GULLY

from Grisedale Tarn

↑ to Keswick

to Penrith & M6 north ↑

Glenridding

Ullswater

Patterdale

Swirral Edge

Red Tarn Crag

Striding Edge

Helvellyn

Thirlmere

Lad Crag
Nethermost Cove

Nethermost Pike

Nethermost Crag

Grisedale

St Sunday Crag

Deepdale

N

0   1   2km
0   1 mile

A591

Falcon Crag

62

Tarn Crag

Grisedale Tarn

Dunmail Raise

Fairfield

Scrubby Crag

60

Hart Crag

Dovedale

A592

↑ to W'mere

to Ambleside ↓

56 Dove Crag

63: GOUTHER CRAG

(a) Truss Buttress (VD) 40m
(b) Kennel Wall (VD) 35m
(c) The Fang (S+) 40m   (d) Sostenuto (VS+) 40m

Summary: A diverse collection of short, high quality routes in an ideal setting. Enough climbing is described for a short day.

First Ascent: Truss Buttress – Ron Fiddler and Eric Arnison, August 1933. Kennel Wall and The Fang – Jerry Williams, Charlie Wilson, Tommy Nicholson and Bob Ewin (with G.H. Tyson on Kennel Wall), October 1946. Sostenuto – Harold Drasdo, Brian Evans, Jack Soper and Pat Harris, August 1959.

Best Conditions: North-west facing at 350m. A quick-drying crag that is often worth considering when other areas are wet.

Approach: Via the A6 to Shap. From the north end of the village turn off west (signed to Bampton and Haweswater) and follow this road, ignoring several turn-offs, until a turn left, signed to Rosgill.

Take this and the next very sharp left, signed to Swindale, and follow the unfenced road to a cattle grid where a tasteful slate notice advises lack of parking space further on. This is almost true, and at busy times cars should be left here and the road followed on foot until just before the farm where a footbridge crosses the stream (parking for four vehicles only at this point). Cross the bridge and follow the path towards the crags over a second bridge. The dramatic ridge above you is Truss Buttress. The other routes are all on Fang Buttress, the next major crag on the right. GR:515 127. 15mins.

Starting Point: Refer to diagram.

Descent: To the right from each buttress (on Truss Buttress scramble over the top of the buttress before attempting to descend).

Time and climbers seem to have passed by the gentle valley of Swindale. Not surprising really – the bleak approach hardly evokes visions of a host of golden daffodils. And yet it is a forgotten gem of Lakeland climbing.

Truss Buttress needs no description beyond 'follow your nose'. It is remarkably consistent at its standard and provides an excellent outing. The same can be said of Kennel Wall, though by contrast it is steep and enclosed. It is with the Fang, however, that Gouther really begins to show its teeth. The thin crack to gain the first belay looks more like *Mild Extreme* than *Hard Severe*, and the whole route has an unremitting feel to it. In fact Sostenuto, though technically a great deal harder, seems little more demanding once the initial problem of getting off the ground has been sorted out.

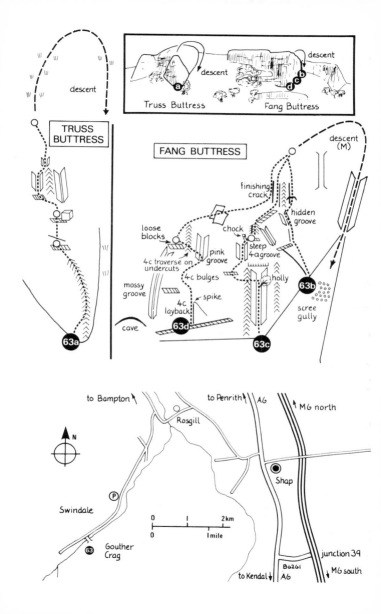

TRUSS BUTTRESS

FANG BUTTRESS

descent

descent

descent

a

Truss Buttress

d

c b

Fang Buttress

descent (M)

finishing crack

hidden groove

loose blocks

chock

4c traverse on undercuts

steep 4a groove

pink groove

4c bulges

holly

mossy groove

63b

4c layback

spike

scree gully

cave

63d

63c

63a

N

to Bampton

to Penrith

A6

M6 north

Rosgill

Shap

Swindale

P

0   1   2km

0   1mile

Gouther Crag

63

to Kendal

A6

B6261

junction 39

M6 south

Langdale

Although popular, Langdale has many hidden corners that the world and its dog pass by in ignorance. The cliffs of Bowfell and Neckband, for example, provide brilliant and unforgettable routes of great character. The drawback of Pavey Ark on a hot bank holiday is the attraction it holds for drunken yobs with their blaring electronic 'music', and this vast but vegetated cliff is not especially prepossessing on first acquaintance. Yet concealed amidst the heather are some great climbs – true mountaineering. But the pride of Langdale has to be the magnificent Gimmer which, with its scrumptious rock, southerly aspect and fine routes of all grades, is indubitably a cut above all other crags in the valley. Lastly to White Ghyll, an impressive and exciting place to climb and, for those to whom such things are important, little more than a stone's throw from the nearest pub.

Approaches: Most people will approach from Ambleside on the A593, turning off on to the B5343 at the Skelwith Bridge Hotel. Follow this road through Chapel Stile until the New Dungeon Ghyll Hotel appears on the right. There is a large car-park just past the hotel. Further up the valley is a second hotel, the Old Dungeon Ghyll where there is a smaller car-park. Several buses run daily from Ambleside.

Accommodation: *Camping*: There is a large campsite near the head of the valley almost opposite the Old Dungeon Ghyll Hotel, and a smaller one at Chapel Stile.
High camps/bivouacs: The best are near the tarns; Stickle Tarn for Pavey Ark and Angle Tarn for Bowfell. Flat ground can also be found between the Pikes above Gimmer Crag, where the source stream of the Dungeon Ghyll is a generally reliable source of water.
Youth Hostels: High Close, Chapel Stile (GR:338 052), Elterwater (GR:327 046), and Ambleside (GR:376 032).
Hotels:There are many guest houses and hotels in the valley (and in Ambleside, which is within reasonable travelling distance) but it is advisable to book in advance during peak periods – the Accommodation Bureau in Church Street, Ambleside (tel. 053 94 2582) and the Tourist Information Centre, Windermere (tel. 096 62 6499), can advise.

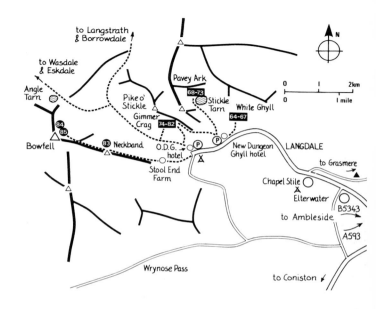

Services: The Stickle Barn bar at the New Dungeon Ghyll Hotel does bar meals and has a cafeteria as well, whilst snacks and meals can be got from the Old Dungeon Ghyll. There is a small shop on the main campsite and other stores at Chapel Stile and Elterwater. The main shopping centre is Ambleside, which also has two good climbing shops (Frank Davies's and Rock and Run) and numerous pubs – The Golden Rule being popular with climbers. There is also a small climbing wall (details from Rock and Run or The Golden Rule). The nearest petrol station is at Chapel Stile. The nearest 24 hour petrol is at Canal Garage, Crooklands (on the A65 where it passes under the M6 north of Junction 36).

Nothing to breathe but air,
  Quick as a flash 'tis gone;
Nowhere to fall but off,
Nowhere to stand but on. . . .

From *The Pessimist* by Ben King (1857–94), quoted by
Showell Styles in *The Mountaineer's Weekend Book* (1950).

64: (a) Laugh Not (HVS) 40m
(b) Slip Knot (VS−) 40m

Summary: Grooves and rooves predominate, the latter avoided by excitingly airy traverses. The main groove on Slip Knot is overcome by some fine climbing up the right wall − a marvellous pitch at this grade. That on Laugh Not, however, must be taken direct on poor jams.

First Ascent: Slip Knot − Jim Birkett and Len Muscroft, May 1947 (the original traversed some 3m lower; the route described was done by John Cook, Jack Haines and J.G. Ball, September 1947). Laugh Not − Joe Brown, Ron Moseley and Tom Waghorn, October 1953.

Best Conditions: Refer to Route 65.

Approach: From the right of the New Dungeon Ghyll Hotel a path crosses a stream and goes through a small gate to a stile over a wall on the right. Take this and continue between the bottom of a wood and a stone wall to a stony clearing. This is White Ghyll. Struggle up it to a sycamore growing in the ghyll-bed at the Lower Crag. GR:297 071. 20mins.

Starting Point: The first major feature encountered is the large and smooth pink overhung corner-groove of Laugh Not. It is reached by very careful scrambling. Just left of Laugh Not, near to the sycamore, is the conspicuous capped corner of Slip Knot. Start at its foot. (Refer also to Route 65 diagram.)

Descent: Refer to Route 65.

Laugh Not is such a good line that it is astounding it had not been climbed prior to 1953. But perhaps it needed the king of jamming to succeed. With modern gear the main groove may no longer test your bottle, but it will certainly test your technique. At its top a roof bars the way − unless you wish to try the direct finish at 5c. Mere mortals traverse rightwards to gain the finishing groove. The pioneers took tension across the slab at this point. Clean of lichen it now goes free, but a better alternative is to reach over the roof and hand traverse right on jugs (further doses of bottle are helpful here) − feet on the slab for the tall, pedalling the air for the not so.

Slip Knot gives similar adventure at a more reasonable grade, though here too the traverse needs thought (and a blind lurch out to the left rib).

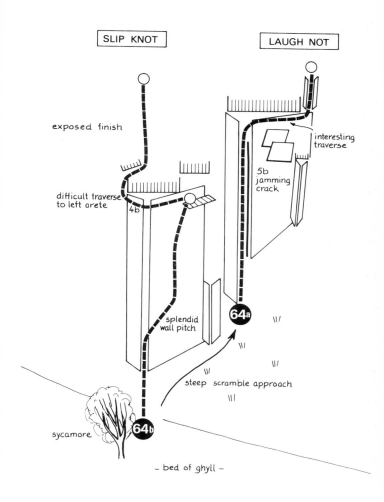

SLIP KNOT

LAUGH NOT

exposed finish

interesting
traverse

5b
jamming
crack

difficult traverse
to left arete

4b

splendid
wall pitch

64a

steep scramble approach

64b

sycamore

– bed of ghyll –

65: WHITE GHYLL WALL (VS–) 70m

Summary: A brilliant upper section is the making of this route. Exposure and 'sporting' protection upset a logical assessment of the technically reasonable climbing.

First Ascent: Jim Birkett, Len Muscroft and Tom Hill, May 1946.

Best Conditions: South-west facing at 300m. Forming one wall of a gully makes White Ghyll slow to dry but also quite sheltered, so whilst prolonged rain will cause seepage from cracks and general greasiness, it can recover quickly after showers. Often in the shadow (due to the far bank of the ghyll) it can be rather windy and cold and is best visited on a warm summer's evening.

Approach: Refer to Route 64. Further up the ghyll, beyond the sycamore, a large area of broken ground gives way to the impressive Upper Crag.

Starting Point: The first major feature encountered on the Upper Crag is a rather broken, rightward-slanting rib with a small tree near its top. Start at the foot of this rib.

Descent: Cautious descents can be made at either end of the crag. That at the upper end, via a shallow scree gully and slope, is the safest in bad weather. Alternatively one can descend the broken ground in between the Upper and Lower Crags.

The rib is nothing – merely the least evil way of getting to the first belay, from where the real climbing begins. Most parties are hard pressed to get off the ledge, the problem being a seemingly innocent scoop which comes too soon, surely, to be the crux. Success leaves an aftertaste of nervous adrenalin that sends one scurrying for good runners before proceeding further.

Nothing looks less like *VS* than the little red wall that follows, and many are stranded here awhile casting about for the 'correct line'. In the end most return to the place they first thought of, and, sooner or later, and often by hook or by crook, gain temporary haven in the broken niche above, adrenalin still flowing freely.

Although the climbing difficulties now ease, the exposure and route-finding problems intensify. There is little to distinguish the correct traverse from the equally likely (but treacherous) lines above and below. Several false starts are the norm before reaching a highly desirable ledge. Do not be surprised at the sense of deliverance as one emerges blinking from an hypnotic hormonal revery.

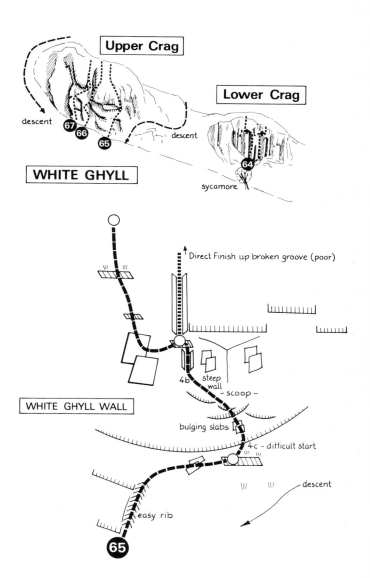

Upper Crag

Lower Crag

descent

descent

WHITE GHYLL

sycamore

67 66 65

64

↑ Direct Finish up broken groove (poor)

4b

steep
wall

- scoop -

WHITE GHYLL WALL

bulging slabs

4c - difficult start

descent

easy rib

65

66: THE GORDIAN KNOT (VS) 70m

Summary: A highly exciting route. Due to exceptional exposure and barely adequate protection, the crux can seem much harder than its grade would suggest.

First Ascent: Jim Haggas and Elaine Bull (later Mrs Haggas), September 1940.

Best Conditions: Refer to Route 65.

Approach: Refer to Route 64. Further up the ghyll, beyond the sycamore, an area of broken ground gives way to the impressive Upper Crag.

Starting Point: To the left of the start of White Ghyll Wall (Route 65), a narrow slab runs directly up to the main overhang (this is about 20m right of White Ghyll Chimney). Start at the foot of the slab. (Refer also to Route 65 diagram.)

Descent: Refer to Route 65.

Jim Haggas led just two new routes in the Lake District, and yet both were breakthroughs in the climbing terms of the late 1930s and early 1940s. His first, Hangover, climbed a very bold and direct line on an area of Dove Crag that had been previously dismissed as impossible. The following year he repeated the procedure at White Ghyll, putting up the well-named Gordian Knot – the first climb to tackle the impending central wall.

The ascent itself was something of an epic. An attempt to clean the route whilst climbing resulted in an impasse on the second pitch where, in Haggas's words, 'the traverse terminates at a widening of the ledge where it is possible to sit with chin in hand surveying the problems to come.' (It is still possible to do so today, and in fact such a sight is not uncommon!) 'The problems' are an intricate series of boulder-problem moves. Even without the covering of moss and loose stones that Haggas found, these are as puzzling as one is likely to meet anywhere at this grade. On one of Haggas's many attempts at this section, he managed to reach a hand ledge to his right, but then found himself penduluming bodily over the void. It was with difficulty that he recovered his footholds and, one presumes, his composure.

Eventually, after some cleaning from above, the route succumbed to a very bold and committing lead – which remains the only way to succeed on it today.

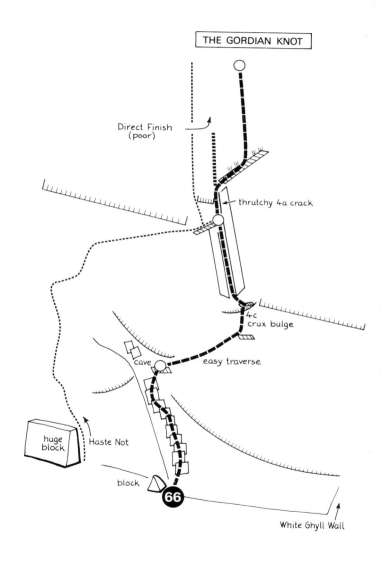

THE GORDIAN KNOT

Direct Finish
(poor)

thrutchy 4a crack

4c
crux bulge

cave

easy traverse

huge
block

Haste Not

block

66

White Ghyll Wall

67: HASTE NOT (VS) 70m

Summary: A tremendous route that wends its way up the steep central area of the crag, finding natural breaks in the overhangs. Comments concerning exposure are as for Gordian Knot (Route 66).

First Ascent: Jim Birkett and Len Muscroft, May 1948.

Best Conditions: Refer to Route 65.

Approach: Refer to Route 64. Further up the ghyll, beyond the sycamore, a large area of broken ground gives way to the impressive Upper Crag.

Starting Point: In the recess to the left of Gordian Knot (Route 66), beside a large boulder and under a wide, slabby wall.

Descent: Refer to Route 65.

The second ascent of Gordian Knot was made by Jim Birkett in 1944 and marked the start of his interest in the cliff. For the next five years he and Len Muscroft dominated White Ghyll, producing many marvellous routes (a selection of which can be found on the previous pages).

Haste Not dates from the end of this period and is one of the best. Like Gordian Knot it is an airy route on very steep ground, but it is easy to be lulled into a false sense of security by the spacious stance and large holds at the beginning of the second pitch. Be warned: neither last for long, and the top pitch is also very problematic. On the first ascent, Birkett made the first delicate moves on this final section and then struggled out of balance for a few seconds. Fearful watchers in the gully were certain he was going to fall. Then suddenly he was up and shouting to them, 'Did you see that? I reached for a bloody hold, but there wasn't one there at all. Thought I was off. Never laughed so much for years.'

I hope you've got as good a sense of humour – that vital hold still isn't there!

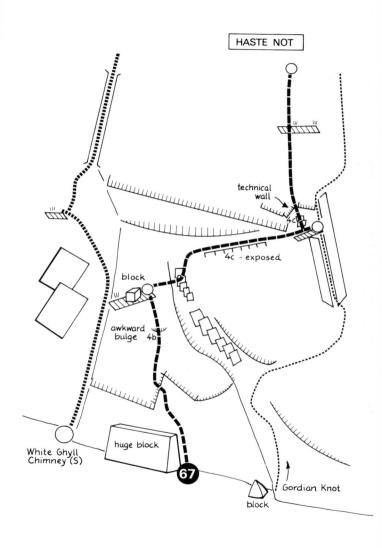

HASTE NOT

technical
wall

4c

4c - exposed

block

awkward
bulge   4b

huge block

White Ghyll
Chimney (S)

67

block

Gordian Knot

68: GREAT GULLY (D or III) 300m

Summary: An interesting series of traditional problems. The whereabouts of the crux depends on prevailing conditions. (Little Gully, to the left, is *M* in summer and *III* by the left branch in winter. The right branch is easier.)

First Ascent: Walter Parry Haskett Smith, 1882.

Best Conditions: South facing at 700m. Good ice is slow to appear and seldom lasts.

Approach: It is best to park in the National Trust car-park adjacent to the New Dungeon Ghyll Hotel. From the back of the car-park follow the course of Stickle Ghyll to Stickle Tarn. Skirt the tarn on its left to scree below the crag. Excepting Brown Tongue, this is probably the most unpleasant approach walk in the Lakes. Jack's Rake (E) slants across the crag from top left to bottom right, dividing the South Face diagonally, and providing a convenient means of descent. GR:286 080. 35mins.

Starting Point: Great Gully is the pronounced deep cleft near the left-hand side of the crag. It contains a huge chockstone. Start at the foot of the cleft.

Descent: Jack's Rake is the usual descent but can be serious in winter. Alternatively an easy continuation gully of two pitches leads to the summit of the crag.

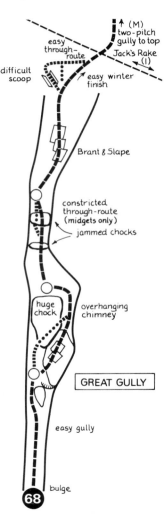

(M) two-pitch gully to top

easy through-route

Jack's Rake (I)

difficult scoop

easy winter finish

Brant & Slape

constricted through-route (midgets only)

jammed chocks

huge chock

overhanging chimney

GREAT GULLY

easy gully

68

bulge

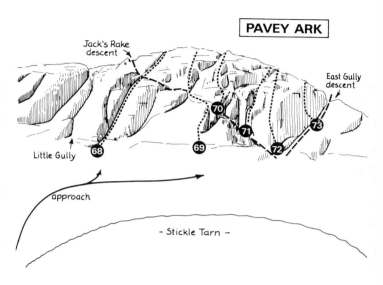

From here either follow the descent directions to Easy Gully (refer to Route 70) or make a wide detour around either edge of the crag.

Tastes in climbing change, much as they do in all things, and what a century ago rapidly became a popular route scarcely sees a summer ascent these days. Not that the quality of Great Gully has altered in any way – in fact this is precisely its problem. On the first ascent the 'Brant and Slape' ('steep and slippery' in Cumbrian dialect) was found to be 'lubricated by a film of fine mud' and, climbing it over a decade later, Owen Glynne Jones concluded (correctly) that 'such was its usual condition'. Definitely not the place for lurex tights.

But it's a different matter in winter when the frost is hard. Now, though the difficulties are greater, the gully takes on a clean, crisp whiteness. The Brant and Slape goes easily on perfect placements, though chimneying the enormous chockstone can be a slippery problem. Incidently, the tights are still best left at home.

69: (a) Arcturus (HVS) 90m
(b) Golden Slipper (HVS) 70m
(c) Poker Face (E1) 70m

Summary: Fine climbing, at its best on a sunny day. (Note: a thin line sling helps protect the crux of Poker Face.)

First Ascent: Golden Slipper – Allan Austin and Brian Evans, June 1958. Arcturus – Austin and Eric 'Matey' Metcalfe, April 1962. Poker Face – Austin and Ken Wood, July 1966.

Best Conditions: South facing at 700m. The initial slabs of Arcturus can be very slow to dry – allow four dry days in summer. Golden Slipper and Poker Face dry more quickly.

Approach: Refer to Route 68 approach and diagram. From the foot of Jack's Rake, traverse left under the lower buttress until below a two-tiered black slab. The wall above the slabs has a triangular overhang at its lower right-hand end.

Starting Point: In a line with the triangular overhang, where a short grassy slab leads to a break/ledge below the bulge which guards the crux slab.

Descent: Via Jack's Rake or Easy Gully (refer to Route 70).

Lakeland climbing entered the doldrums in the late 1950s. Birkett and Greenwood had retired; Peascod had emigrated; and Dolphin was dead. Ross was active but largely confined to Borrowdale. The fells awaited a new man to take up Dolphin's tragically fallen banner. That man was John Allan Austin.

Austin, like Dolphin, made significant advances at Almscliffe with impressive solo first ascents of Wall of Horrors (E3,5c) and Western Front (E2,5c). Like Dolphin, he too climbed throughout the Lakes (but made his major contributions in Langdale), and over the next twenty years his name became synonymous, as had Dolphin's before him, with the highest standards on rock. Three of his most notable efforts are presented here.

It is best to start with Arcturus, as this lands one on Jack's Rake quite close to the start of Golden Slipper. But take heed that the slab on the first pitch is hard and protected only by two dubious pegs – not good news if your legs take time to warm up. Golden Slipper is itself a sustained lead on excellent gabbro-type rock. It is adequately protected by wires though this was not always so and it still retains something of a reputation. The independent first pitch of Poker Face is repulsive and it is better to abseil down from a good spike at the top of the Slipper to climb it as a slightly harder variation.

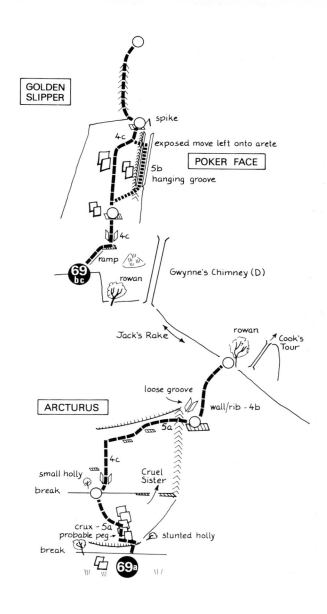

70: COOK'S TOUR (D+) 100m

Summary: An enjoyable climb with some good grazing. Large stances and short pitches (those indicated on the diagram can easily be split), coupled with impressive situations, make this a suitable and rewarding route for beginners. It can be combined with an ascent of Great Gully (Route 68), followed by a partial descent of Jack's Rake, for a long and interesting excursion.

First Ascent: Jack Cook and G.B. Elliott, March 1943.

Best Conditions: South facing at 600m. Dries quickly in summer.

Approach: Refer to Route 68 for the crag approach and to locate the foot of Jack's Rake. Scramble up the rake, passing under Rake End Chimney (Route 71). The rake now steepens; continue until it eases again. On the left now is a strong rowan, on the right a short off-width crack leading to a pinnacle.

Starting Point: At the foot of the off-width crack.

Descent: Either locate the top of Jack's Rake (not easy on first acquaintance) and descend this, or go over the back of the crag into a natural fault line containing a well-worn trail. Follow this down to the right to a col on the right. This gives access to Easy Gully (M), the wide scree gully under the East Face.

Cook's Tour, with its easy sunny climbing, comfortable stances, and outstanding views out over Langdale to Windermere and Morecambe Bay, provides ample opportunity for quiet reflection on the beauty of its surroundings – green fields and oak woods, gills, tarns and lakes, the timeless old grey walls, and the splendid grandeur of the high fells. Most of what can be seen lies within the boundaries of the National Park, and a constant battle is fought to maintain its appearance of rural peace. One can only hope that your grandchildren will take your great-grandchildren up Cook's Tour and still be able to enjoy the same simple pleasures.

'Jack's Rake. On page 63 of the 'Langdale Book' it is stated that the first recorded ascent of this course was made by Jack, circa 1400 A.D. Will any member possessing evidence of any previous ascent kindly communicate with the editor?' G.S. Bower, 'Climbs Old and New', *Fell & Rock Journal* (1921).

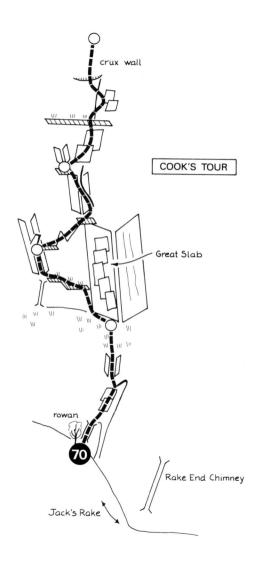

crux wall

COOK'S TOUR

Great Slab

rowan

70

Rake End Chimney

Jack's Rake

71: (a) Rake End Chimney (D+) 80m
(b) Rake End Wall (VS) 70m
(c) The Rib Pitch Finish (HVS) 40m

Summary: The chimney is a classic of its type; steep and exposed in the lower half, with interesting climbing above. It is exasperating when wet. Rake End Wall is a highly satisfying traditional VS with the option of a harder finish on the Rib Pitch (on which 'Friends' or similar devices improve the protection).

Best Conditions: South facing at 700m. Allow one dry sunny day in summer, two for The Rib Pitch.

Approach: Refer to Route 68 for the crag approach and to locate the foot of Jack's Rake. Go up the rake a few metres but stop before it steepens. Rake End Chimney is the first chimney encountered.

First Ascent: Rake End Chimney – Claude Barton, October 1898. Rake End Wall – Arnold Carsten and Ernie Phillips, August 1945. The Rib Pitch – Allan Austin and Jenny Ruffie (later Mrs Austin), June 1958.

Starting Point: Rake End Chimney – scramble up into the chimney. Rake End Wall – 5m to the right of the chimney (the first challenge will be to gain a protruding block by a rising traverse to the left).

Descent: Via Jack's Rake or Easy Gully (refer to Route 70).

Cumbria, the land of the Cymry or Welsh Celts, is rich in tradition. The name Pavey Ark probably derives from a mixture of old Norse and Gaelic: *Pavia's Ergh* – a summer hut among high pastures (belonging, one must assume, to Pavia – 'The Morose One').

These three climbs are diverse in style and history, but all are good and share a fine setting above Stickle Tarn. Rake End Chimney is typical of its kind for a rope length, until a well-placed chockstone is overcome. The upper pitches are more gully-like and eventually peter out altogether amidst the rock and heather of the summit. From here, calm water might allow a glimpse of the submerged remains of an old stone hut – a mystery shimmering beneath the surface of the tarn.

Pavey Ark has always lagged behind compared with developments on other large crags in Lakeland. Rake End Wall was a magnificent but late discovery by a man more noted for his Welsh explorations. Varied and intricate, its standard and stature can be increased by taking the Rib Pitch to finish.

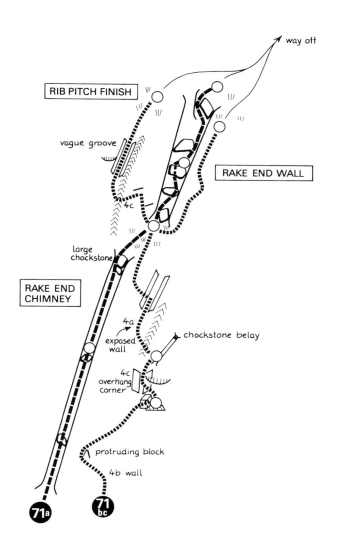

RIB PITCH FINISH

way off

vague groove

RAKE END WALL

4c

large
chockstone

RAKE END
CHIMNEY

4a
exposed
wall

chockstone belay

4c
overhang
corner

protruding block

4b wall

71a

71
bc

72: STOAT'S CRACK (S+) 125m

Summary: A long climb of great variety. The crux is both difficult and exposed.

First Ascent: B.R. Record and John Jenkins, June 1933.

Best Conditions: South facing at 600m. Allow one dry day after rain.

Approach: Refer to Route 68 for crag approach and to locate Jack's Rake.

Starting Point: At the very foot of Jack's Rake, under the left-hand end of a heather ledge.

Descent: Refer to Route 70.

Stoat's Crack is what is usually described as 'a good mountaineering route'. What this means exactly is not certain, apart from the fact that the climb in question is usually to be found on a mountain. However, the phrase does conjure up a pleasant vision: a long and intricate climb with large belays and a low order of difficulty; where enjoyment comes more from the experience of the whole rather than the solution of its parts; and where the route is included as part of a full mountain day — ideally culminating in the ascent of a summit. It is usual to travel light on such an itinerary: one rope, little gear, and a good weather forecast being the generally agreed requirements. This is a very good way to do Stoat's Crack, though you may find yourself needing all of your runners and wishing for a few more on the deceptive groove of the main pitch. Thankfully it is easier now than on the desperate first ascent, when grass and mud on the sloping holds led to a VS grading.

As for the mountain. . . well, there's Pavey itself, or a traverse round to Harrison Stickle where the rest of the day can be lazed away in sunbathing and bilberry picking — and possibly just the occasional shaded glance back at the crag to trace the line of a very fine and enjoyable climb.

'Mountains seem to exercise a very disturbing influence on our accurate observation of fact.' — L.J. Oppenheimer, *The Heart of Lakeland* (1908).

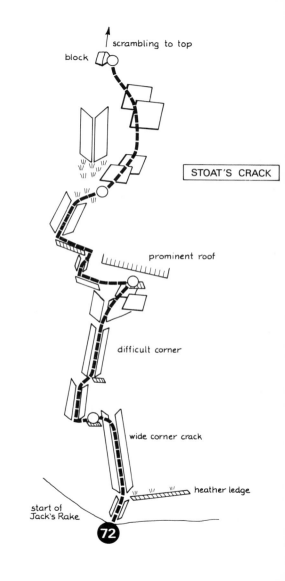

scrambling to top

block

STOAT'S CRACK

prominent roof

difficult corner

wide corner crack

heather ledge

start of
Jack's Rake

72

73: ASTRA (E2) 100m

Summary: A magnificent lead, one of the hardest in this book, requiring good technical ability and a steady nerve.

First Ascent: Allan Austin, Eric 'Matey' Metcalfe and David Roberts, May 1960.

Best Conditions: East facing at 600m. Allow two dry days in summer. The final short V-groove is often wet.

Approach: Refer to Route 68 for the crag approach. From the foot of Jack's Rake, go round to the right and up the scree of Easy Gully under the imposing East Face. Where the scree is split by a grassy rock rib follow the left-hand gully branch.

Starting Point: About halfway up the left gully branch, under some bulging slabs. (These can be climbed by several means until a hand traverse leads into a short corner on the left.)

Descent: Make an upwards detour to the right and then across right to join a good path. Follow this down to the right to a col at the top of Easy Gully (M) and descend this. Alternatively descend via Jack's Rake as for Route 70.

One climbs in exalted company on Astra. To left and right – taking the far more obvious lines – are harder, more modern climbs. Yet if anything this adds to the spirit of this great route, one of Austin's finest.

It starts innocently with a vague line up the slabs and wall of Hobson's Choice (ridiculously steep for *Severe*). This lands one on a large sloping ledge at the foot of an open-book corner. This is Eclipse (E4), a route which saw many attempts before it finally succumbed in 1976. Austin went right here, and so shall we, creeping round the arête with a move that seems impossible until a hidden pocket is discovered, allowing a cautious drift out to a comforting spike. The scoop above is not as hard but lacks runners and is very exposed; a resting place allows a resumption of respiration.

To the right is a thin and ragged vertical crack. Austin hung from a piton here on the first ascent, but now it provides good nut protection. It is the key to a very delicate move right where the difficulties close with delightful suddeness. The pitch beyond is superb too – a meandering groove of dreamy rock and severe space. Being easier, it lacks the bite and uncertainty of the crux, allowing some slight and well-deserved relaxation in truly awesome surroundings.

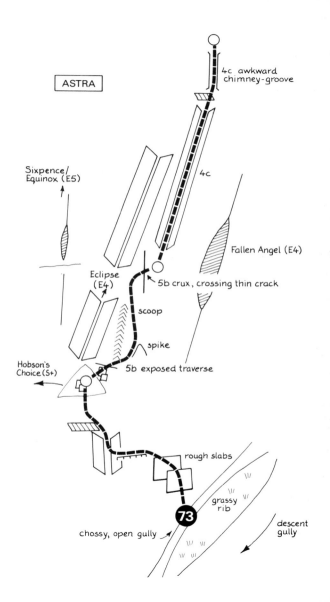

ASTRA

4c awkward chimney-groove

Sixpence/
Equinox (E5)

4c

Fallen Angel (E4)

Eclipse
(E4)

5b crux, crossing thin crack

scoop

spike

5b exposed traverse

Hobson's
Choice (S+)

rough slabs

grassy
rib

descent
gully

chossy, open gully

73

GIMMER – APPROACHES AND DESCENTS

Approaches: 1a   From the Old Dungeon Ghyll Hotel. Cross a stile behind the hotel and strike up the hillside between two walls. After 100m branch left over another stile. Zig-zag up scree and hillside to an escarpment on the left which is followed to the crag. GR:277 070. 45 mins.
1b   You can also continue from the first stile and follow a good level track until directly under the crag which is reached laboriously up steep bracken (simplest but most unpleasant).
2   From the New Dungeon Ghyll Hotel. A path to the east rises to ford the Dungeon Ghyll below Dungeon Ghyll Force. It now zig-zags steeply to a plateau where Harrison Stickle can be seen ahead. Just before it begins to rise steeply again, a subsidiary track descends left over the escarpment to the South-East Face of the crag. 1hr.

Descents: 1   To the right of Gimmer Chimney (Route 74) is the huge South-East Gully. This is easy but serious if wet.
2   It is almost as quick to make a detour round the right edge of the crag.
3   Junipall Gully, on the left side of the crag, is the other side of the fault line which forms South-East Gully. It is harder and looser but has the advantage of returning to the north-west side. The lower section of the gully is avoided by rock ribs on the left (looking out).
4   Junipall Gully can be avoided by a wide detour back and to the left of the crag.

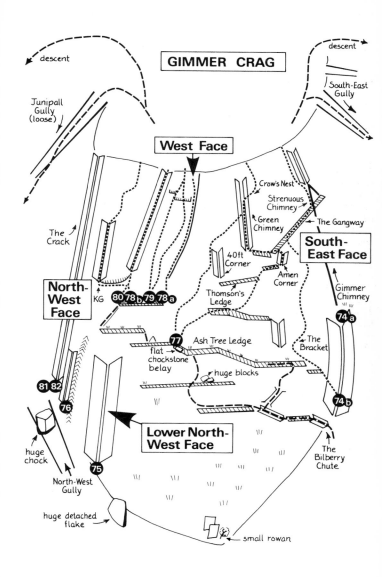

North-West Arête (Route 76b).
  (Photo: Stephen Reid.)

Kipling Groove (Route 80).
  (Photo: Steve Ashton.)

74: (a) **Gimmer Chimney (VD) 90m** 08/07/07
(b) **Bracket & Slab (S) 100m**

Ash, Phil

Summary: Nicely long, lower-grade routes on the 'tourist's side' of the crag. Perfect rock and stupendous situations throughout. Bracket and Slab is S+++ if the Strenuous Chimney is included (protection is available but awkward to arrange on this pitch).

First Ascent: Gimmer Chimney – E. Rigby, John Sandison and Andrew Thomson, November 1902. Bracket & Slab – Harry Lyon, Jack Herbert, Mabel Barker, Herbert Porrit Cain and Jack Wilton, August 1923 (the Strenuous Chimney was first climbed by Harry Kelly and J.B. Meldrum in May 1918).

Best Conditions: South-east facing at 500m, and quick to dry. Both routes are climbable in most con-

ditions (with the exception of the Strenuous Chimney pitch, which takes a day or two to deslime itself and is 'Hard Very Ridiculous' when wet).

Approach: Refer to 'Gimmer Approaches', page 180.

Starting Point: The line of Gimmer Chimney is marked by twin cracks that run practically the entire height of the South-East Face. Start from a mound at the base of the right-hand crack, gained by scrambling up a short, easy V-groove from the path. Bracket & Slab starts at a pointed flake, below and to the left, at the bottom of the V-groove.

Descent: Refer to 'Gimmer Descents', page 180.

Gimmer Chimney is much more interesting than the average climb of this designation, with steep slabs initially and a tricky traverse to follow. Admittedly there is an overhanging off-width in the middle, but the direct continuation up the Strenuous Chimney is avoided by a hidden gully on the right.

The Strenuous Chimney is reserved for Bracket and Slab (though unscrupulous parties have been rumoured to avoid it). It caused Lyon, 'an hour's hard struggle, disastrous to skin and clothes,' and left him with but 'a very hazy recollection of the methods employed, except that they were distinctly unpleasant.' He thought Amen Chimney might be a suitable name for it.

For all that, the real delight in Bracket and Slab is the unique traverse of the Bracket itself and the elation of discovering the neatness of the Neat Bit. Traditionalists may scoff, but it is not terribly difficult to convince oneself that the easier right-hand variation is more in keeping with the rest of the route.

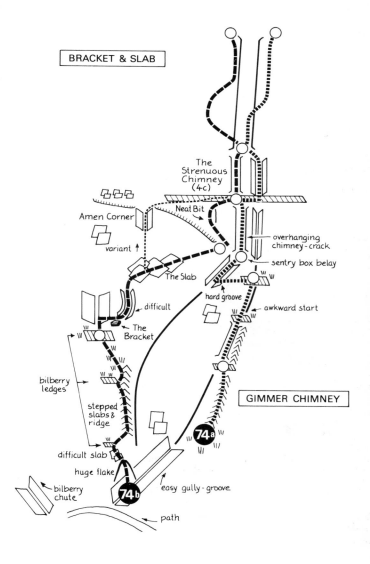

BRACKET & SLAB

The
Strenuous
Chimney
(4c)

Neat Bit

Amen Corner

variant ↑

The Slab

overhanging
chimney - crack

sentry box belay

difficult

hard groove

The Bracket

awkward start

bilberry
ledges

stepped
slabs &
ridge

GIMMER CHIMNEY

74a

difficult slab

huge flake

74b

bilberry
chute

easy gully - groove

path

75: (a) Ash Tree Slabs (VD+) 50m
(b) Ash Tree Corner (VS+) 50m

Summary: Two good ways to Ash Tree Ledge. Protection is poor on the crux of the Corner, hence the grading.

First Ascent: Ash Tree Slabs — George Bower and Arthur Wakefield, June 1920. Ash Tree Corner — Rick and Jenny Graham, April 1981.

Best Conditions: North-west facing at 500m. Ash Tree Slabs dries quickly in a good breeze, but the Corner can remain damp for a week.

Approach: Refer to 'Gimmer Approaches', page 180.

Starting Point: 20m up the hillside from a huge, detached flake (shown on 'Gimmer Approaches' diagram) is a prominent corner, its right-hand side being formed by a wide, attractive slab. Both routes start at the foot of the corner.

Descent: By ascending one of the West Face routes (refer to Routes 77, 78, 79 & 80); or, if you really must, by descending the Bilberry Chute (refer to diagram accompanying 'Gimmer Descents', page 180.

The sad thing about Gimmer (probably the *only* sad thing about Gimmer), is that its greatest asset, the magnificent West Face, doesn't quite reach the bottom of the crag. Thus classic climbs like 'C' Route and Oliverson's are only half as long as they ought to be. To almost remedy this situation it is necessary to visit what was once known (until Nancy Ridyard ticked it all) as the 'Gentleman's Side'.

Here will be found a selection of short routes ending where the West Face climbs begin. Put them together imaginatively and Ash Tree Ledge barely intrudes. Asterisk and 'D' make a perfect match, while North-West Arête and K.G. share the same 'way out there' feel.

Of these two climbs, Ash Tree Slabs has delighted for decades and is the ideal entree for any of the alphabet routes — the 'soup and fish' of Bower's 'full course'. It is beautifully exposed and a little delicate; as much a joy to second as it is to lead. Its companion was, until recently, that almost mythical thing: a totally overlooked corner crack on a popular crag. The odd dollop of damp moss testifies to the freshness of the first ascent, but does not detract from the trueness of line. It is merely the price one pays for a classic in the making.

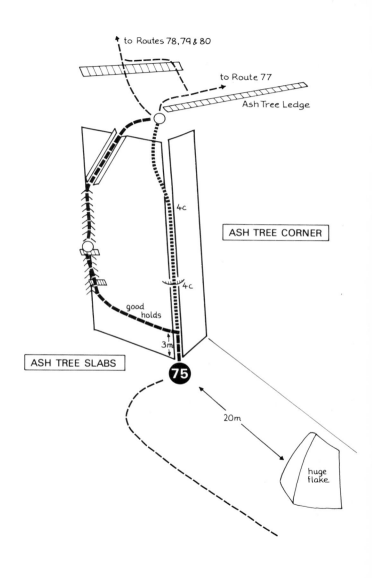

to Routes 78, 79 & 80

to Route 77

Ash Tree Ledge

4c

ASH TREE CORNER

4c

good holds

3m

ASH TREE SLABS

75

20m

huge flake

76: (a) Asterisk (S+) 45m
(b) North-West Arête (VS–) 45m

Summary: Both routes give brilliant and well-protected wall climbing to the Ash Tree Ledge. A shame they are so short. North-West Arête is a little artificial.

First Ascent: Asterisk – Herbert Gross, George Basterfield and Bryan Tyson, May 1928. North-West Arête – Jim Birkett and Vince Veevers, September 1940.

Best Conditions: Despite being north-west facing at 500m, the wall dries quickly in summer. Allow one day.

Approach: Refer to 'Gimmer Approaches', page 180. Traverse under the toe of the crag to the north-west side, and ascend to the prominent corner of Ash Tree Slabs (Route 75). Continue up North-West Gully to an enormous chockstone, the top of which makes a good lounging area. Level with this, an unpleasant looking corner defines the left edge of the area in question.

Starting Point: From just right of the corner, scramble on to a narrow, rightwards-slanting ledge, at the base of the overhung wall.

Descent: By ascending one of the West Face routes (refer to Routes 77, 78, 79 & 80); or, if you really must, by descending the Bilberry Chute (refer to diagram accompanying 'Gimmer Descents', page 181).

Asterisk, it is said, derives its name from rhyme:

He who leads this terrible wall,
  'as ter risk an awful fall.

Times have changed since 1928 and, though the climb is no less steep, the risk is minimal now. It was a line Basterfield would have spotted during his guidebook excursions, and with Gross to the fore it must have seemed a pushover after their Dow climbs.

Basterfield, at one time Mayor of Barrow-in-Furness, was a father figure to many youngsters in the close-knit climbing community of the 1920s. A noted extrovert he was capable of some marvellous feats – such as his solo of Intermediate Gully in seven and a half minutes. But perhaps his most surprising achievment was in getting G.S. Bower, who once signed himself 'Grievously Startled Bachelor', to marry his daughter! This too was commemorated in verse:

The toughest pitch of all will yield,
  When assailed by Basterfield.

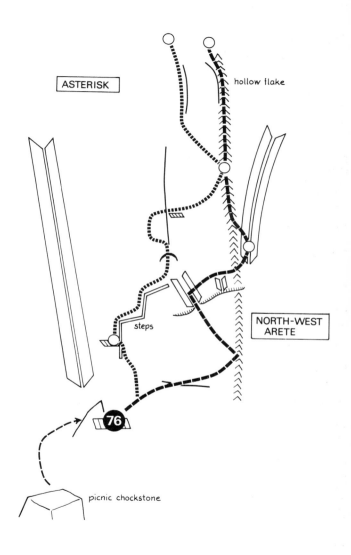

ASTERISK

hollow flake

NORTH-WEST
ARETE

steps

76

picnic chockstone

77: **WEST FACE CLASSICS**

(a) 'A' Route (VD+) 70m
(b) 'B' Route (S−) 60m (c) 'C' Route (S) 65m
(d) Oliverson's Variation and Lyon's Crawl (VD) 60m

Summary: If these routes have a fault (and it must be their only one) it is that their various pitches can be interchanged at will. Superb rock. Excellent situations. Scattered protection.

First Ascent: 'A' Route – E. Rigby, Darwin Leighton and John Sandison, April 1903. 'B' Route – Harry Lyon, Jonathon Stables and Andrew Thomson, July 1907. 'C' Route – A.P. Wilson, G.H. Jackson and A. Bundritt, August 1913. Oliverson's Variation – C.H. Oliverson, G.C Turner and F.B. Kershaw, May 1907. Lyon's Crawl – Lyon, Stables and Thomson, on the same day.

Best Conditions: South-facing at 500m, and very quick to dry.

Approach: Refer to 'Gimmer Approaches', page 180. Gain Ash Tree Ledge, either by scrambling up the Bilberry Chute or by climbing a route on the Lower North-West Face (refer to Routes 76 and 77).

Starting Point: Oliverson's Variation starts at the highest point of the right-hand section of Ash Tree Ledge. 'A', 'B' and 'C' Routes start from a flat chockstone two metres to the right. A large platform will be seen on the skyline up to the right.

Descent: Refer to 'Gimmer Descents', page 180.

Although Haskett Smith had visited Gimmer in 1882 and climbed South-West Gully, the crag remained strangely neglected until the turn of the century, when Rigby and Thomson began explorations. Gimmer Chimney was theirs, likewise 'A' Route. Rigby also named and led the infamous corner where 'the devout second will sympathetically murmur "Amen" to any remarks let fall by his leader whilst struggling. . .' The rest of the party had to be hauled; and it was another team who eventually incorporated 'Amen Corner', as it came to be known, into the popular 'B' Route. The remarks quoted are from the first guide to Gimmer, produced by George Basterfield. In it he also described 'C' Route as 'a very interesting climb and as full of good things as a Christmas pudding.'

Thus beganeth the 'Alphabet'. With continuously steep climbing, excellent rock, and a feeling of 'fresh air all the way', its component characters have been understandably popular with each succeeding generation of climbers.

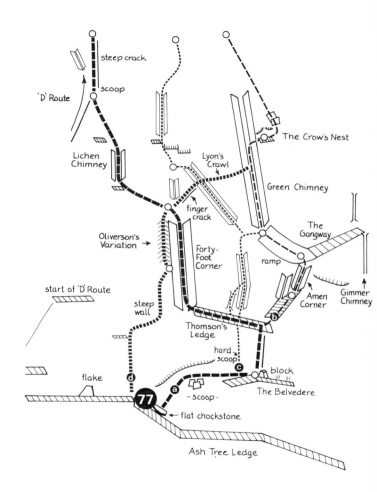

78: (a) 'D' Route (S) 35m
(b) 'F' Route (VS) 45m

Summary: A pair of excellent crack climbs with sound protection. Difficulties vary considerably according to the hand jamming proficiency of the climber.

First Ascent: 'D' Route – George Bower and P.R. Masson, May 1919. 'F' Route – Jim Birkett and Vince Veevers, May 1941.

Best Conditions: South-west facing at 500m. 'D' Route dries quickly; allow half a day in summer. 'F' Route takes longer due to seepage; allow three dry days.

Approach: Refer to 'Gimmer Approaches', page 180. Both climbs start from the upper left-hand end of Ash Tree Ledge. Although this can be gained via the Bilberry Chute, a better approach is to climb one of the Lower North-West Face routes (refer to Routes 75 and 76).

Starting Point: Hanging above the left-hand end of Ash Tree Ledge is a prominent corner groove that extends from the beginning of the Kipling Groove traverse to the top of the crag. This is 'F' Route – start in a line below the groove. To the right of 'F' Route the rock is very smooth with a band of high overhangs (Whit's End Direct and Spring Bank, Route 79). Right again it becomes more broken. 'D' Route climbs more or less up the junction of the rough with the smooth, starting on the uppermost ledge under an overhanging triangular recess.

Descent: Refer to 'Gimmer Descents', page 180.

For some, gritstone is the only rock worthy of the name; for others, it is sheer purgatory. Whatever your standpoint, it has to be acknowledged that a disproportionate number of our greatest climbers have had considerable gritstone experience. George Bower was no exception, and he put his knowledge to good use in the Lakes where his ascent of 'D' Route heralded a resurgence in Lakeland climbing following the void of the Great War.

Confused parties are commonplace on the jumble of the West Face, but beyond the first overhang 'D' runs straight as a die, following a crack of Peak District-like character and aspiration. For those who are fond of grit it provides a hundred feet of unadulterated bliss.

The overhanging left wall of 'F' Route ensured that it remained inviolate for a later generation. It too succumbs to a Black Rocks technique, but the strenuous crux comes right at the top. If it is true that you can judge jamming ability by the scars you haven't got, then 'F' is the place to put your hands to the test.

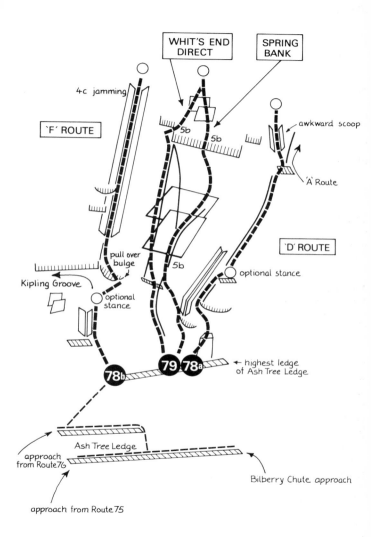

79: (a) Whit's End Direct (HVS+) 45m
(b) Spring Bank (E1) 45m

Summary: A fine matched pair of sustained slab climbs. Protection is good where it matters most, but the final roofs ensure the outcome is always in doubt. (Illustrated on Route 78 diagram.)

First Ascent: Whit's End Direct – Allan Austin and Rod Valentine, October 1972. Spring Bank – Mike Mortimer, Ed Cleasby, Marjorie Allen, Mike Lynch and Jeff Lamb, June 1979.

Best Conditions: South facing at 500m, and very quick drying.

Approach: Refer to 'Gimmer Approaches', page 180. Both climbs start from Ash Tree Ledge. Although this can be gained via the Bilberry Chute, a better approach is to climb one of the Lower North-West Face routes (refer to Routes 75 and 76).

Starting Point: At the upper left end of Ash Tree Ledge. A wide, smooth slab, capped by a long roof, is set between the groove of 'F' Route on the left, and the crack of 'D' Route on the right. Whit's End Direct starts below a short left-slanting crack that leads to a thin crack-line running up to the left-hand end of the roof. Spring Bank begins just left of 'D' Route below a vague scoop.

Descent: Refer to 'Gimmer Descents', page 180.

These are modern routes in every way. Short, sharp and to the point, they seem incongruous amongst the cracks and grooves of this most traditional of crags. But good slab climbs are scarce in Lakeland, and here are two of the best.

Both seem hard from the start, and they get harder still on reaching the thin cracks of the main slab. Difficulties finally merge into one continuous crux that intensifies slightly as respective roofs are overcome. There are no rests in the eaves, but the initial protection – though strenuous to fix – is brilliantly solid. Not so on the upper wall, where the runners give out just as the holds appear and force an unprotected lead to the top on rapidly expiring strength.

Of the two, Spring Bank is slightly more sustained; but both grades are 'top-end', and anyone setting off with the idea that it will all be easy going until a quick 'one, two, and over' will be in for a long, slow shock.

Whit's End Direct (Route 79a).
  (Photo: Steve Ashton.)

80: KIPLING GROOVE (HVS) 50m

Summary: A milestone in any climber's career. Although its reputation for seriousness has long gone, its reputation as a magnificent climb is deservedly undiminished. (Illustrated on Route 82 diagram.)

First Ascent: Arthur Dolphin and John Lockwood, May 1948.

Best Conditions: West facing at 500m. The first pitch can weep for several days after prolonged rain.

Approach: Refer to 'Gimmer Approaches', page 180. Start from Ash Tree Ledge. Although this can be gained via the Bilberry Chute, a better approach is to climb one of the Lower North-West Face routes (refer to Routes 75 and 76). North-West Arête (Route 76) provides an exciting and logical start.

Starting Point: To the left of the upper left-hand end of Ash Tree Ledge is a wide slab capped by a prominent long overhang, beneath which runs a horizontal off-width crack. From a start on Ash Tree Ledge, the first pitch begins by climbing up left to gain this crack.

Descent: Refer to 'Gimmer Descents', page 180.

Many had 'looked' at this obvious line over the years, and in fact it was Birkett who gardened it by abseil. But Dolphin, busy preparing the new Langdale guidebook, stepped in and top-roped it before making a clean lead. Even with this prior knowledge it was a daunting run-out, with the hard climbing forty feet out from his last sling. Dolphin called the climb Kipling Groove because he considered it 'Ruddy 'ard', and he was right.

Kipling Groove starts half-way up the crag with a curious traverse left on undercling holds. When attacked boldly this gives no trouble, but take care to prevent ropes jamming once the stance has been gained. The groove above leads to an airy step right on to the face and a few moves up bring the crux within reach. You can tell it's the crux because of Joe Brown's peg. It's not really Joe Brown's peg of course, but it was he (feeling that the run-out wasn't justified) who first placed one here during the third ascent. Opinion was against him and the peg has been removed on numerous occasions since. Funny, then, that it should still be there. You also know this is the crux because the smooth flow of activity inexplicably falters. That is, until a rapid succession of rightward fingery moves lead the way to huge jugs, a short groove, and a great sense of achievement.

81: THE CRACK (VS) 80m

Summary: Though first classified as 'unpleasantly severe', The Crack is now one of the best routes in the valley. It gives tremendous climbing and good protection on excellent Gimmer rock. Highly popular. (Illustrated on Route 82 diagram.)

First Ascent: Arthur Basil Reynolds and George Graham Macphee, May 1928.

Best Conditions: North-west facing at 500m but, like most Gimmer routes, it dries quickly in summer.

Approach: Refer to 'Gimmer Approaches', page 180. Go around the toe of the buttress to gain the North-West Face, and go up North-West Gully to an enormous chockstone (good picnic spot). Up to the right is the well-defined corner of The Crack which extends to the full height of the cliff.

Starting Point: The lowest section of The Crack curves down into an easy-angled wide groove. This forms the first pitch – start at its foot.

Descent: Refer to 'Gimmer Descents', page 180.

There are but a few climbs so imposing that they are honoured by being named prior to their first ascent. Cenotaph Corner and Great Wall spring to mind. The Crack likewise.

That it would be climbed one day was not in doubt. The only question was, by whom? Bower and Basterfield had both made roped reconnaissances from above, but in those days The Crack was filled with turf and so was a harder and less attractive proposition. In the event it was A.B. Reynolds, another of the very few climbers then operating at these limits, who made the historic ascent. Reynolds was particularly noted for his barefoot climbing exploits (which included Murray's in winter, and Central Buttress), and an extraordinary leader fall on Scafell which caused Basterfield's thumb to be severed by the thin alpine line they were using. It was his second attempt, following a benightment and subsequent top-rope rescue the previous month. Much gardening had been undertaken in the intervening period.

The route itself is quite stunning. Devious and tricky in the lower half, with a technical wall traverse and awkward mantelshelf, it assumes a straightforward, almost gritstone, simplicity once the Bower is attained; 'The Crack' says it all.

82: GIMMER STRING (HVS+) 85m

Summary: A magnificent eliminate on perfect rock. The technical crux is superbly protected. At the upper limit of the grade.

First Ascent: Allan Austin, Eric 'Matey' Metcalfe and Dave Miller, July 1963 (first complete ascent).

Best Conditions: North-west facing at 500m. Quick to dry.

Approach: Refer to 'Gimmer Approaches', page 180, and then approach as for The Crack (Route 81).

Starting Point: As for The Crack (Route 81).

Descent: Refer to 'Gimmer Descents', page 180.

Thus named by Austin because he did not make the first ascent so much as string all the bits together, Gimmer String is a climb that dithers in that pleasantly hard area at the very top of the HVS grade. So prepare yourself mentally for *Extreme* and get going: it's easier that way.

The start up the first section of The Crack allows a warm up, and no real difficulty will be encountered until reaching the top of the pedestal. Here those foolish enough to wear shorts discover that the chimney above the roof has gritstone teeth. One pops up, hopefully not too badly savaged, on to easier slabs (where a good race for the stance can be had with leaders on Kipling Groove).

The next pitch is absolutely outstanding, with some of the best positions on Gimmer. The groove of Kipling Groove is relinquished for the left arête. This is climbed, magnificently, way out from The Crack, to a well-deserved rest below the final, impending wall. Here excellent runners can be fixed (many of them, if wished). But they should provide no physical assistance at all for those final precarious bridging moves so essential to success.

'It is no solution at all to fail, and then to go round to the top and abseil down to place a fixed piton and hanging sling which can be reached from below, in order to by-pass a particularly troublesome spot.' J.A. Austin and R. Valentine, *Fell & Rock Guide to Langdale* (1973).

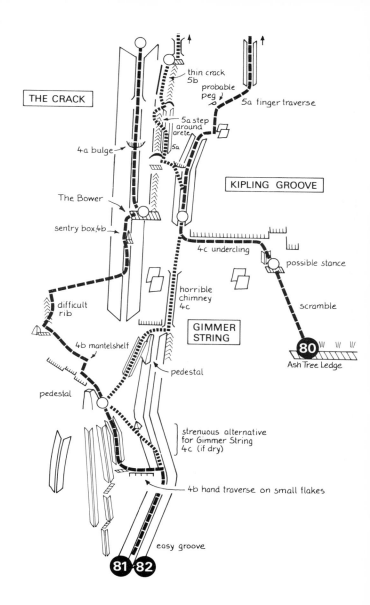

THE CRACK

thin crack
5b

probable
peg

5a finger traverse

5a step
around
arete

5a

4a bulge

KIPLING GROOVE

The Bower

sentry box, 4b

4c undercling

possible stance

difficult
rib

horrible
chimney
4c

scramble

4b mantelshelf

GIMMER
STRING

80

Ash Tree Ledge

pedestal

pedestal

strenuous alternative
for Gimmer String
4c (if dry)

4b hand traverse on small flakes

easy groove

81 82

83: NECKBAND CRAG

(a) Mithrandir (HVS) 40m
(b) Gandalf's Groove (E1) 40m
(c) Razor Crack (HVS) 80m (d) Gillette (E2) 40m

Summary: Excellent, sustained one-pitch climbs on good rock.

First Ascent: Gandalf's Groove – Allan Austin and 'Comic Pete' Jenkinson, July 1964. Razor Crack – Austin and Ken Wood, August 1966. Gillette – Wood and Austin, July 1968. Mithrandir – John Hartley and Rick Sager, August 1972.

Best Conditions: North facing at 600m and extremely slow to dry. Allow at least two virtually dry summer weeks.

Approach: Best approached by ascending the smooth tongue of land known as the Band which divides upper Langdale. Park at the Old Dungeon Ghyll and walk along the main valley road for a few minutes until it turns sharp left. A farm track leads to Stool End Farm at the foot of the Band. Go through the farmyard and follow the footpath slightly left of the ridge to the plateau at the top of the Band. Descend north-east (right) to the crag, which is just below the summit. GR:261 061 and marked on some maps as Earing Crag. 50mins.

Starting Point: Refer to the diagram opposite.

Descent: Directly to the left side of the crag, precariously.

Gandalf's Groove was the first of the harder routes to be climbed on Neckband Crag. It involves delicate rib and wall climbing, with a few moves of high technical difficulty. It has since been superseded by Mithrandir which strenuously tackles the groove avoided by its predecessor. Surprisingly, Mithrandir is not only a better route but is actually slightly easier.

Razor Crack takes a determined line up a ferocious wall relieved only by overhangs. Fortuitous jugs above each and every roof means that it goes at a remarkable *HVS* (a word of warning: it was originally graded *Extreme*, and only the protection has changed).

Gillette follows the same route as far as the first roof, where thin moves left gain an elegant subsidiary groove in the arête. It is low in its grade, not particularly strenuous; and the protection is reasonable. Taken confidently it is the most enjoyable of all.

For the energetic, a continuation up the Band to climb Sword of Damocles (Route 84) will complete an excellent mountain day. And if you don't make it to the Golden Rule before closing, you're just not fit.

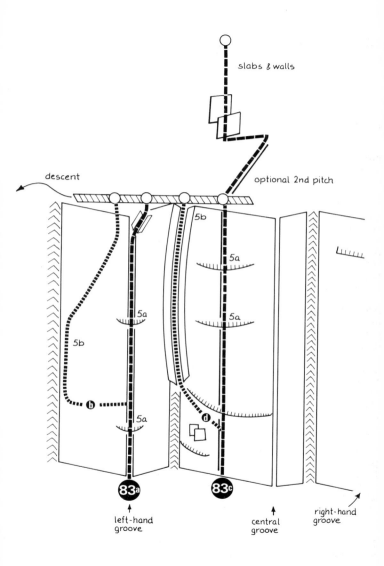

slabs & walls

descent

optional 2nd pitch

5b

5a

5b

5a

5a

b

d

5a

83a

83c

left-hand
groove

central
groove

right-hand
groove

84: SWORD OF DAMOCLES (E1) 60m

Summary: A high mountain route on tremendous rock and in a fine position. Protection is adequate on the crux pitch which, though short, is sustained and awkward.

First Ascent: Pete Greenwood, Don Hopkin and Arthur Dolphin, August 1952.

Best Conditions: North-east facing at 700m. Allow a week of dry weather.

Approach: Follow the approach to Neckband Crag (Route 83) as far as the summit of the Band. Continue until the path steepens and forks. The right-hand branch climbs steeply up to join the superbly situated Climber's Traverse, passing under several small crags. Follow it rightwards, passing a spring (Bowfell Buttress lies straight ahead) and then scramble up grass underneath the triple-groove buttress of North Buttress. GR:245 069. 1hr 30mins.

Starting Point: Under the right-hand and most prominent groove. Scramble up right and back left to a ledge and short slab cut by a great curving crack. Start at the crack.

Descent: Down the scree shoot to the right which divides North Buttress from Bowfell Buttress.

The fabled Sword of Damocles symbolises the insecurity of happiness. Sadly (or happily, depending on how one views these things) the large poised flake which gave this climb its name succumbed to the laws of gravity around 1978. However, there is still plenty of insecurity to be gained from the two hollow-sounding blocks that remain. Dolphin led the 'Sword' on the first ascent, and it must have been a worrying time for Greenwood and Hopkins on the restricted stance below.

1952 was a good year for all of them: with Greenwood, Dolphin had put up (amongst others) Hell's Groove on Scafell – a route which entered new realms of steepness – whilst with Hopkin he had climbed the excellent line of Trespasser Groove on Esk Buttress.

If you can, climb on Neckband Crag in the morning and then make your way up here mid-afternoon. Wangle the lead of the excellent layback crack of the top pitch and let your partner grapple with the 5b mossy corners and doubtful flakes below. At the top you are but a few yards from the summit of Bowfell with its magnificent view of Scafell's Central Buttress in the dim and distant blue.

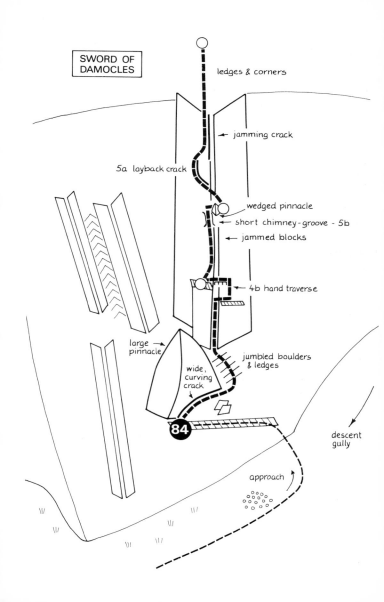

SWORD OF DAMOCLES

ledges & corners

jamming crack

5a layback crack

wedged pinnacle

short chimney-groove - 5b

jammed blocks

4b hand traverse

large
pinnacle

wide,
curving
crack

jumbled boulders
& ledges

84

descent
gully

approach

85: BOWFELL BUTTRESS (D+) 110m

Summary: A long mountaineering route in superlative isolation at the head of Langdale. Harder than implied by the grade in any but the driest conditions. An excellent but difficult winter route when iced (V).

First Ascent: Tom Shaw, G.H Craig, Gerald West, Charles Hargreaves and Lehmann Oppenheimer, May 1902.

Best Conditions: East facing at 700m. Allow three days of good dry weather in summer. A good snow covering together with a prolonged freeze is required in winter.

Approach: Follow the approach to Neckband Crag (Route 83) as far as the summit of the Band. Continue until the path steepens and forks. The right-hand branch climbs steeply up to join the superbly situated Climber's Traverse, passing under several small crags. Follow it rightwards, passing a spring. Bowfell Buttress lies straight ahead across scree. GR:245 069. 1hr 30mins.

Starting Point: Slightly left of the lowest point of the crag, approximately 10m below a short chimney that cuts rightwards into the crag.

Descent: To the left; or, better, continue to the summit of Bowfell and descend via one of the walking routes.

Scan the rugged eastern flank of Bowfell from Langdale and the eye is met by a tumultuous confusion of rock, gill and fell. The only smooth path is straight through the middle where the gigantic flying buttress of the Band props up the hillside. Many a Victorian cragsman must have trodden this way, bound for Scafell or Gable and never dreaming that the crest of the ridge was all that stood between him and one of Lakeland's greatest classics. And so it might have remained had not Shaw and Craig lost their path one foggy day in Rossett Ghyll. But convincing others of their 'huge pillar-like buttress' was not easy, and it was some years before a reluctant party could be persuaded to investigate.

Shaw led and met with a slight setback in the first chimney when a knob of rock caught in the collar of his jacket and sent him back down again. They enjoyed themselves tremendously on the rest of the route. On the summit of Bowfell the others rightly congratulated the innovators on having 'discovered and mastered a first-rate new climb'. But, as Oppenheimer pointed out, 'It was the struggle to attain, not the attainment of the goal, that they had come for.'

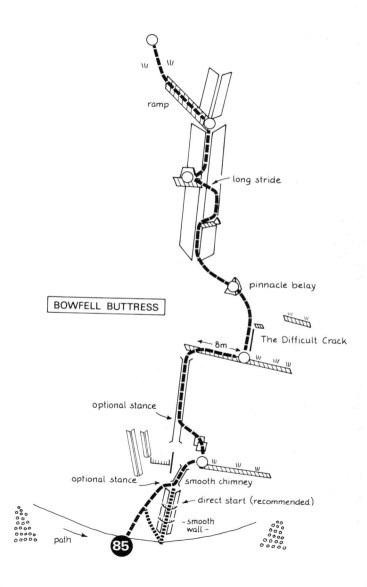

BOWFELL BUTTRESS

ramp

long stride

pinnacle belay

The Difficult Crack

8m

optional stance

optional stance

smooth chimney

direct start (recommended)

smooth wall

path

85

Eskdale

The Eskdale of concern to climbers is the Valley of the Upper Esk. No-one lives here, and not a hint of infernal combustion disrupts the peace. Heron Crag lies only a short distance beyond the last farmsteads, but even here the loudest noise is the tac-tac of the stonechat.

Esk Buttress stands alone in impressive isolation at the head of the valley. Despite the plethora of excellent routes here, the long approach weeds out all but the most enthusiastic teams. It is easy to be over-awed by the vastness of your surroundings: Mickledore hangs high above, with the great bulging bulk of Scafell's East Buttress threatening to burst forth and inundate the combe; while through the haze the startling gash of Cam Spout echoes the distant cry of peregrines. Below the Esk whispers by in gentle meanders. Heaven feels very close on Esk Buttress.

Approaches: The valley lies parallel to Wasdale and comments as to road access, public transport and so on are broadly similar. Approaches to Esk Buttress (GR:225 064, marked 'Dow Crag' on some maps) are as follows:

1 From near Cockley Beck (GR:243 017) on the Wrynose/Hardknott road. This is the quickest approach, but also the least easy to follow in mist. The path begins a short distance to the west of the gated bridge at Cockley Beck Farm. The path, distinct at first, soon becomes lost in the Mosedale bogs. Follow the valley for its full length and continue in the same line, crossing Lingcove Beck at a dogleg above a waterfall. Skirt the highest outcrops on their left, following a line towards Mickledore. More bogs drain into the Esk, which is forded to the crag. 1hr.
2 Via Eskdale. Park near Brotherilkeld Farm (GR:212 012). 1hr 45mins.
3 From Wasdale. Follow the Scafell approach as described in the Wasdale area introduction (page 18) and then descend from Mickledore to Esk Buttress. 2hrs 30mins (and VS on the feet).
4 From Seathwaite, Borrowdale, via Grains Ghyll and Esk Hause. 2hrs 15mins.
5 From Langdale via Angle Tarn and Esk Hause. 2hrs 15mins.

Accommodation: *Camping*: Fisherground Farm (GR:152 001), Hollins Farm (GR:178 009) and Brotherilkeld Farm (GR:213 014).
High camps/bivouacs: There are good sites on the bank of the Esk.
Youth Hostels: Boot (GR:196 011) and Black Hall (GR:239 013).
Hotels: Several in Lower Eskdale.
Services: Boot boasts several shops and a Post Office. The nearest pub is the Woolpack, which is convenient for the Youth Hostel.

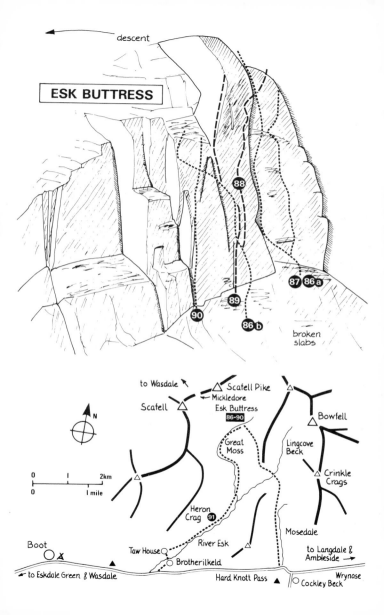

ESK BUTTRESS

descent

88

87 86 a

89

90

86 b

broken
slabs

to Wasdale ↖   △ Scafell Pike
Scafell △   ← Mickledore
                  Esk Buttress
                  86-90

N

△   Bowfell

Great
Moss

Lingcove
Beck

0   1   2km
0   1 mile

△   Crinkle
     Crags

Heron
Crag 91

Mosedale

Boot ○ ✕

Taw House ○   River Esk
        ○ Brotherilkeld

△

to Langdale &
Ambleside →

← to Eskdale Green & Wasdale

Hard Knott Pass ▲ ‖ ○ Cockley Beck   Wrynose

86: (a) Bower's Route (S+) 135m
(b) Bridge's Route (S) 80m

Summary: Great climbs in a magnificent setting. Bridge's, in particular, provides the lower-grade climber with a route as exposed and intricate as any in this book. Bower's is more difficult and slightly vegetated, which makes it trying in the wet. (Bower's Route is illustrated on Route 87 diagram.)

First Ascent: Bower's Route – George Bower, Arthur Wakefield, and P.R. Masson, May 1920. Bridge's Route – Alf Bridge, Alan Bennet Hargreaves, Maurice Linnell and William Dyson, July 1932.

Best Conditions: South-east facing at 500m. Dries quickly after showers and, being low-lying, often misses the bad weather attracted by Scafell. Allow two dry days after prolonged rain.

Approach: Refer to the area introduction.

Starting Point: The main face is guarded by a band of broken, vegetated slabs over which various scrambles give access to the routes proper. For Bower's, go up scree to the right of the slabs until a grassy rake slants up left to a good ledge. Bridge's starts from a square ledge slightly left of centre of the area dominated by the crag's vast central pillar. (Note: up to the left of this ledge is a square chimney.) Refer also to the crag diagram in the area introduction.

Descent: Various precarious paths lead down very steep ground on the left of the crag. The safest descent, and almost as quick, is simply to walk over the back of the crag and descend steep grass to the left.

Bower's Route was the first on this impressive but remote crag. Claude Frankland and Bentley Beetham made the second ascent, avoiding the overhanging chimney by an even more difficult crack on its left. It was nine years after Bower when Colin Kirkus and 'A. B.' Hargreaves finally made the third ascent. It was wet and they too avoided the dripping chimney, this time by a short detour to the right.

The pace of development was gradual in those days, when there were scarcely two dozen hard climbers active in the county. So 'A. B.' was able to wait a further three years before he recruited his party and walked over from Langdale on a fine day of bright skies. Their intention was the inspiring red pillar that towers over the crag: but they were forced out left. It is hard to believe that such a brilliant route as Bridge's was born out of failure.

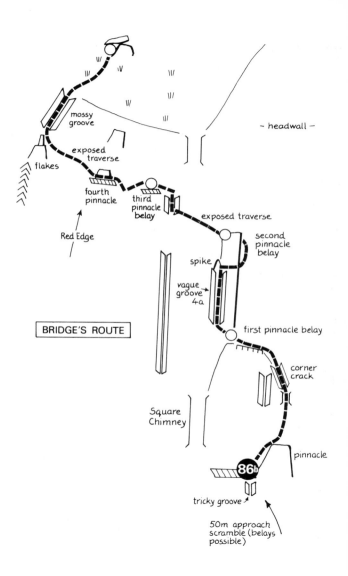

BRIDGE'S ROUTE

mossy groove

- headwall -

exposed traverse

flakes

fourth pinnacle

third pinnacle belay

exposed traverse

Red Edge

second pinnacle belay

spike

vague groove 4a

first pinnacle belay

corner crack

Square Chimney

86

pinnacle

tricky groove

50m approach scramble (belays possible)

87: TRESPASSER GROOVE (HVS) 145m

Summary: A good long climb, trespassing upon the edge of Central Pillar, and posing an interesting variety of problems. Though strenuous, it is well protected and not particularly difficult for the grade.

First Ascent: Arthur Dolphin and Don Hopkin, September 1952 (Frankland's Crack was climbed by Claude Frankland and Bentley Beetham in the 1920s).

Best Conditions: As for Route 86.

Approach: Refer to the area introduction.

Starting Point: As for Bower's Route (Route 86a). Refer also to the crag diagram in the area introduction.

Descent: To the left of the crag (refer to Route 86).

Trespasser Groove, although hard and modern, has the atmosphere of an older and more rambling route. It is easy to imagine the leader struggling with both the difficulties and a continual barrage of good-natured banter from friends gathered at the belay. The climbing is great fun and makes a complete day in itself for those not in a hurry.

Trespasser Groove is a good route, too, if you suffer from a climbing partner who sulks when not getting all the hardest leads. Exercise the gentle art of gamesmanship and innocently offer up two of the three 5a pitches and you will then be out in front on the splendid long groove of the main pitch. Meanwhile your partner's 'hard' leads prove to be a rope-length of grass, a one-move wonder, and the fearsome Frankland's Crack. Given that Frankland was famed for his bold leads of strenuous, overhanging, gritstone jamming cracks, and that this one seems to have been transported straight from Almscliffe, the banter is usually loud and prolonged.

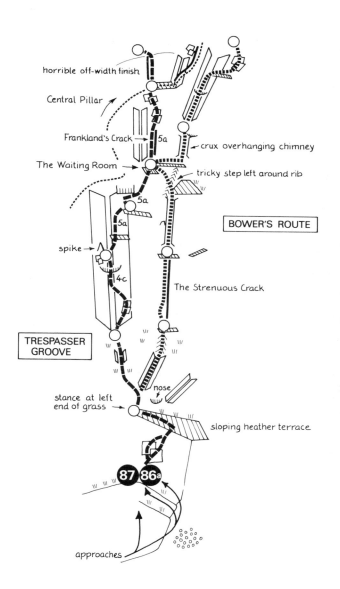

horrible off-width finish

Central Pillar

Frankland's Crack → 5a

crux overhanging chimney

The Waiting Room →

tricky step left around rib

5a

5a

BOWER'S ROUTE

spike →

4c

The Strenuous Crack

TRESPASSER
GROOVE

nose

stance at left
end of grass →

sloping heather terrace

87 86a

approaches

88: CENTRAL PILLAR (E2) 110m

Summary: A thrilling climb that builds up to a superb crescendo on the strenuous penultimate pitch, where the holds are big, flat and rattly. Protection is barely adequate. Technical difficulty is not particularly great but a bold approach is essential. Frightening positions.

First Ascent: Peter Crew and Mike Owen, June 1962 (the direct start was added by Rick Graham and Andy Hyslop in July 1977).

Best Conditions: As for Route 86.

Approach: Refer to the area introduction.

Starting Point: As for Bridge's Route (Route 86b). Refer also to the crag diagram and the area introduction.

Descent: To the left of the crag (refer to Route 87).

Central Pillar had defeated all and sundry – Bridge, Birkett and Dolphin among them. Loose blocks on the crux headwall had become the *mauvais pas* – until Soper abseiled down and cleaned the pitch for Austin. But an unguarded remark in the Old Dungeon Ghyll soon reached long 'Welsh' ears; Peter Crew made an unsportsman-like dawn raid and snatched the plum.

Taking the modern start, the real work begins from the pinnacle of Bridge's. A vague crack points the way up superb bubbly rock to the traverse of the original route. Now the slabs rear up in two steps, each of which provides considerable interest and exposure. These are not well protected and are easy only by comparison with the ludicrous offering that follows.

From an uncomfortable stance, a cliff-hanger ledge (of the B movie variety) soon narrows to nothing as the rock bulges menacingly. Breathe out, topple gently to the right, lunge up for a good hold – and you are either at the peg or off. Somewhere behind your left ear now, a highly suspect block must be grabbed, taped, hauled at, and stood upon. Search at full stretch for the jug – not where it looks to be, but where it ought to be. The holds here are flat and large enough to be called a ledge, but the rock ahead overhangs; secured by nothing more than a poor wire at foot level, this is no easy resting place. Take heart: just a few more moves, either up or sideways, and it's cracked.

From the sunny bay of the belay, the overhanging flake to the summit should prove no problem at all.

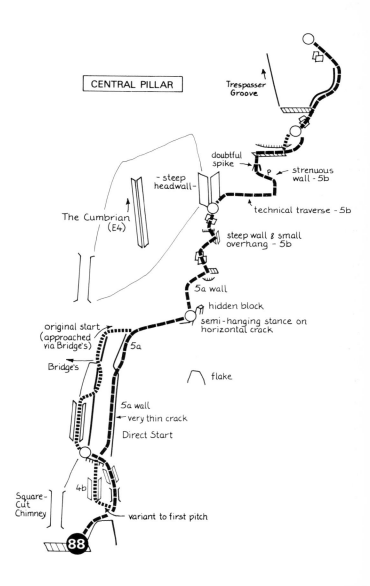

CENTRAL PILLAR

Trespasser Groove

doubtful spike

strenuous wall - 5b

technical traverse - 5b

steep headwall

The Cumbrian (E4)

steep wall & small overhang - 5b

5a wall

hidden block

semi-hanging stance on horizontal crack

original start (approached via Bridge's)

5a

Bridge's

flake

5a wall

very thin crack

Direct Start

Square-Cut Chimney

4b

variant to first pitch

88

89: (a) Medusa Wall (VS) 110m
(b) Great Central Start (VS) 50m

Summary: Fine *VS* climbing with the tremendous Medusa Wall Arête Finish. The Great Central Start is harder but highly recommended. Protection is good throughout.

First Ascent: Great Central Climb – Jim Birkett and Tom Hill, July 1945. Medusa Wall – Arthur Dolphin and Joe Griffin, August 1947.

Best Conditions: As for Route 86.

Approach: Refer to the area introduction.

Starting Point: Scramble up vegetated slabs below the Central Pillar. Start both routes from a ledge below and right of Square Chimney, as for Bridge's Route (Route 86b). Refer also to crag diagram in the area introduction.

Descent: To the left of the crag (refer to Route 86).

There is something slightly disappointing about Esk Buttress *VS*s. Comparisons with Bridge's or Central Pillar leave them wanting in both quality and continuity. Yet, with a little ingenuity, there is some excellent climbing to be had. The best combination by far is to start up Bridge's then quit it for the main pitch of Great Central Climb. A steep wall gets steeper before a demanding mantelshelf allows you to breathe freely again. A few jugs and a short traverse lead to the second pinnacle stance on Bridge's.

Medusa Wall gains the same spot more directly, but take the crack just right of Bridge's to prolong both difficulty and enjoyment. Again, don't follow the traverse of Bridge's to the bitter end but instead launch up a testing jamming crack that lands one exhausted in the upper chimney.

The fine Arête Finish is fitting reward for the labours below.

'There was the usual choice of handholds – loose rock or grass. I chose the grass. It would, at least, give way with less abruptness.' Arthur Dolphin, *Fell & Rock Journal* (1948).

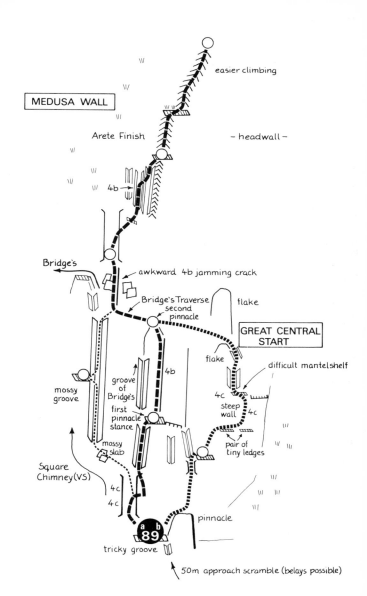

MEDUSA WALL

easier climbing

Arete Finish

– headwall –

4b

Bridge's

awkward 4b jamming crack

flake

Bridge's Traverse
second
pinnacle

GREAT CENTRAL
START

groove
of
Bridge's

4b

flake

difficult mantelshelf

mossy
groove

4c
steep
wall

4c

first
pinnacle
stance

mossy
slab

pair of
tiny ledges

Square
Chimney (VS)

4c
4c

a b
89

pinnacle

tricky groove

50m approach scramble (belays possible)

90: RED EDGE (E1) 80m

Summary: Though low in technical difficulty for the grade, this fine route is sustained. Protection is adequate but some of the holds could be sounder.

First Ascent: Allan Austin, Jack Soper and Eric 'Matey' Metcalf, June 1962.

Best Conditions: As for Route 86.

Approach: Refer to the area introduction.

Starting Point: Left of the start of Bridge's Route (Route 86b) is a large wall, bounded on its left-hand side by the V-shaped Frustration Chimney. Start at the bottom of the chimney (the climb quits this after a few metres for the reddish grooved rib on the right).

Descent: To left of the crag (refer to Route 86).

One can imagine the horror. After all, it was going to be such a great day. . . Central Pillar – the last-great-problem to beat all last-great-problems – ready and waiting for Austin. But there was that car parked where it shouldn't have been; the hurried slosh across the morning bog; the doom-laden ring of hammer against piton. . . Pete Crew, the * * * *!, and already high on the crag. . .

They found what little solace they could in two new routes that black Sunday. Red Edge is the better and has since become a much sought-after lead. Its off-vertical angle, combined with sustained climbing and sometimes imaginary protection, makes it a suitable *Extreme* for those long on neck but short on muscle. It takes a good line too. All things considered, Austin and his party could have done much worse.

'It is very unwise to dispense with the rope, even on simple courses.'
Owen Glynne Jones, *Rock Climbing in the English Lake District* (1897).

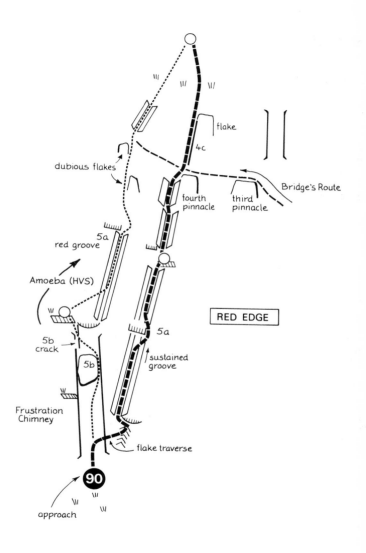

RED EDGE

Bridge's Route

flake

4c

third pinnacle

fourth pinnacle

dubious flakes

5a
red groove

Amoeba (HVS)

5b crack

5b

Frustration Chimney

5a

sustained groove

flake traverse

90

approach

91: GORMENGHAST (HVS+) 80m

Summary: Classic climbing at the upper limit of its grade. Protection is non-existent on the mantelshelf section, and whilst the alternative crack to the right has runners it is also harder. The line of Bellerophon (VS) is indicated for those wishing to fill in the day.

First Ascent: Les Brown and Tony Atkinson, March 1960 (the direct start was added by Allan Austin and Eric Metcalfe in July 1961, and the direct finish by Don Whillans and Albert Ashworth in the same year).

Best Conditions: South-east facing at 200m. Quick drying, unlike the other climbs on this cliff.

Approach: Refer to the area introduction. Park in Eskdale (GR:212 012) near to the driveway of Brotherilkeld Farm. Go to the farm, cross the Esk by a footbridge, and follow a path to Taw House Farm. From here the path contours the river bank northwards to the crag. GR:223 029. 30mins.

Starting Point: Under the clean central buttress, below the shallow groove that bisects the main face.

Descent: To the left of the crag.

At Hardknott, overlooking Eskdale, stand the ruins of the Roman fort Mediobogdum, a name that probably summed up well the feelings of its Dalmation guard. To the north stands Gormenghast, a castle of a different sort.

But our climb has little to do with Mervyn Peake's gaunt and tangled vision of Gormenghast, 'brooding in umbra. . . deep in a fist of stone', for ours is a climb of commitment – and the joy that comes with success born of that commitment. True, like its literary namesake, it has grown patchwork-fashion, improved to perfection by later additions, but that is all. There is no despair here, no 'darkness winding between the characters'. A measured dose of fright, maybe, as each succeeding mantleshelf gives way to a harder one (the last runner receding too far below) and the ecstatic thrill of endless small incuts on a superbly steep finish.

On the battlements of Gormenghast all is sunlit and welcoming. Even the cold wind and the gathering rain clouds seem friendly. In fact the only excuse for gloom is failure to make it to the top.

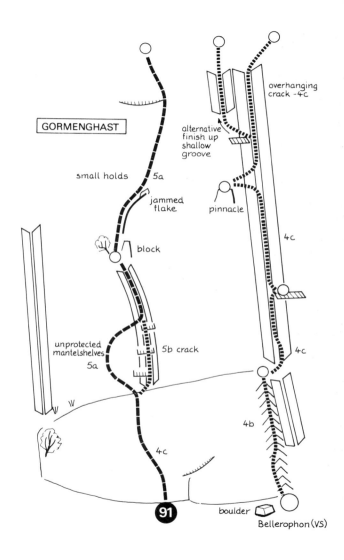

GORMENGHAST

overhanging crack -4c

alternative finish up shallow groove

small holds 5a

jammed flake

pinnacle

block

4c

unprotected mantelshelves

5b crack

5a

4c

4c

4b

91

boulder

Bellerophon (VS)

The Southern Fells

The Southern Fells, like their eastern counterparts, cover a large area, but the two districts have little else in common. Here the barrenness of the East is missing, replaced by gentle valleys, wooded with beech and oak. Small tarns, green pastures and whitewashed cottages complete a perfect picture of rural tranquility.

Yet, around Coniston, one chances on an unexpected moonscape of disused mineworkings and discarded slate. And also Dow, a giant amongst crags, thankfully hidden from the greater part of these industrial intrusions by the welcome bulk of Coniston Old Man. All the climbs in this section are to be found on Dow, and, though they cover the full gamut of grades, only one quality is represented – superb. The rock is of the roughest, the scenery haunting and enchanting, the climbing magnificent.

Approaches to Coniston: 1 From the south via the A590, A5092, A5084 and A593.
2 From the north via the A593 from Ambleside. Weekday bus.

Accommodation: *Camping*: Coniston Hall, 2km south of Coniston (GR:305 965), and at Crook Farm, Torver (GR:287 947).
High Camps/Bivouacs: Good, flat areas along the Walna Scar Track.
Youth Hostels: Far End, Coniston (GR:302 981) and Coppermines Valley (GR:289 986).
Hotels: Many hotels and guest houses in Coniston, and a few in Torver.

Services: Good pubs and cafes in Coniston, and several shops (the nearest climbing shops are in Ambleside). Garages at Coniston and Torver. For 24 hour petrol *see* Eastern Fells.

Crag Approach: From Coniston, follow a metalled road (which leads on to the Walna Scar Track) past the Sun Hotel. It becomes very steep and narrow, and eventually reaches a gate where it branches into two unmade tracks. Park here (or risk a further kilometre). Continue on the left-hand track, around the flank of the Old Man, to a large cairn (the Walna Scar Track goes left here). Go up steep grass and follow a path to the southern end of Goat's Water and the crag. GR:264 977. 1hr.

Alternatively walk from Torver via old quarries. 1hr 30min.

Winter Climbing: Great Gully is grade III and Intermediate a tough IV though seldom in condition. A popular climb is Low Water Beck (III, IV if finished direct) which drains out of Low Water on the northern side of the Old Man (GR:275 983). Above this tarn is a crag which gives good icefalls up the centre (III/IV), and simpler gullies on the left and right.

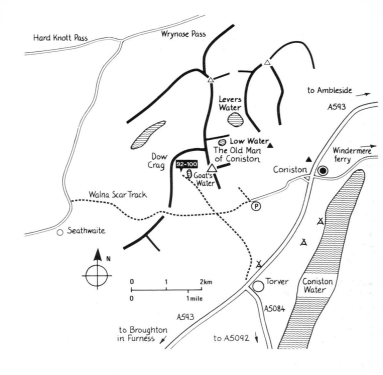

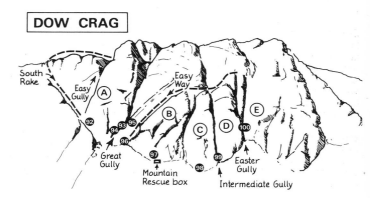

DOW CRAG

South Rake
Easy Gully
(A)
92
93 95
94
96
Great Gully
97
Mountain Rescue box
98
(B)
(C)
(D)
99
100
(E)
Easter Gully
Intermediate Gully
Easy Way

92: (a) Gordon and Craig's Route (S–) 110m
(b) Arête, Chimney and Crack (S–) 115m

Summary: Although the central section is common to both climbs, each is worth doing in its own right. The upper pitches in particular offer tremendous exposure and positions without requiring the climber to use anything smaller than a 'jug'.

First Ascent: Gordon and Craig's – Sholto Hamilton Gordon, Alan Craig and party, September 1909. Arête, Chimney and Crack – T. Clement Ormiston-Chant, T.H.G. Parker and Gordon, September 1910.

Best Conditions: East facing at 700m. Allow three dry days.

Approach: Refer to the area introduction and crag diagram.

Starting Point: The major buttress on the left side of the crag is 'A' Buttress. This imposing face, bristling with overhangs, is bounded on the left by Easy Gully. Arête, Chimney and Crack starts at the foot of the arête defining the left edge of the main face. Gordon and Craig's starts 15m to the right (and a short scramble upwards) at a point where a polished scoop line leads diagonally leftwards to the arête.

Descent: Via South Rake. First scramble to the top of 'A' Buttress then turn left, along the ridge, passing the top of Easy Gully (right-hand branch). Walk over the next short rise (about 200m) to a depression where South Rake leads down into the lower reaches of Easy Gully.

The Fell and Rock Climbing Club was first mooted at Dow and it was founded in 1906 'with the sole object of fostering a love of mountaineering and the pastime of rock-climbing in the English Lake District'. It has successfully pursued that objective ever since.

Gordon and Craig, two of the club's founding members, shared a common desire to find a route up the then virgin face of 'A' Buttress. During an early foray they discovered a spectacular traverse. It would prove to be the key to their eventual success but, lacking a third man, they were forced to retreat. Returning with reinforcements, they found the traverse straightforward but with few belays. At its end, a short slab led to a 'good landing on to apparently loose rocks overhanging the Great Gully in a most imposing fashion'. Craig thought the little corner above 'the stiffest thing in the climb', and most would agree with that.

They had noticed, of course, the great crack that rose up midway along their traverse. Gordon, who had already climbed the Arête on a top rope, returned the following year to complete the equally fine variation of Arête, Chimney and Crack.

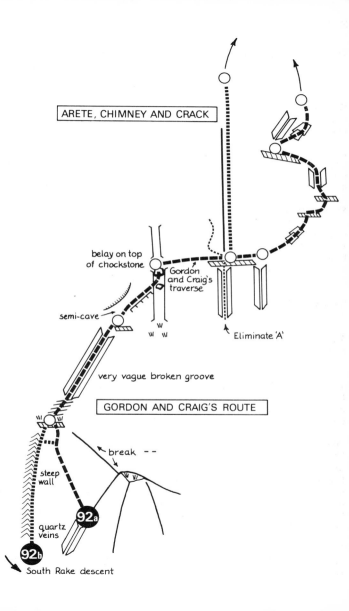

ARETE, CHIMNEY AND CRACK

belay on top
of chockstone

Gordon
and Craig's
traverse

semi-cave

Eliminate 'A'

very vague broken groove

GORDON AND CRAIG'S ROUTE

break --

steep
wall

92a

quartz
veins

92b

South Rake descent

93: ELIMINATE 'A' (VS) 120m

Summary: One of the great routes of its grade, combining a succession of hard, exposed pitches with good stances and magnificent rock. Protection is sparse on the first and last two pitches, and the climbing is continually sustained.

First Ascent: Herbert Gross and George Basterfield, June 1923.

Best Conditions: East facing at 700m. Allow four dry days.

Approach: Refer to the area introduction and crag diagram.

Starting Point: The deep Great Gully divides 'A' and 'B' Buttresses; start 10m up to the left from its base, at a small grass ledge.

Descent: Via South Rake (refer to Route 92).

The first of the Fell and Rock guidebooks, that to Dow Crag, was published in 1922. In it George Bower wrote: 'The Great Wall of "A" Buttress is as yet unclimbed, and appears likely so to remain until the advent of a future race of climbers, fitted with suctorial digits, or unscrupulous enough to make use of fixed ropes.' Naturally, such a challenge could not be ignored; the route was completed – in excellent style – the very next year.

The first pitch, though short, has few good runners and the tenacity required can come as a bit of a shock so soon off the ground. Beyond, magnificent and complex wall climbing leads to a good resting point (but awkward belay) on the pedestal. The next obstacle is the 'Rochers Perchés', a highly technical mantelshelf. A tiny hole in the arête here is worth threading to safeguard the second. The Great Flake then provides an easy handrail through the overhangs, before a delicate and ridiculously exposed traverse leads back across their very lip. The final groove may seem a trifle artificial at first, but it quickly becomes (if you'll excuse the pun) totally engrossing.

Bower made the second ascent of Eliminate 'A', which he enthusiastically praised as, 'Une belle ascension sur l'herbe et rochers perchés.' The plants and poised blocks may have long since departed, but the resulting acreage of clean and sound rock is hardly to the detriment of the climb. It is still very much 'une belle ascension.'

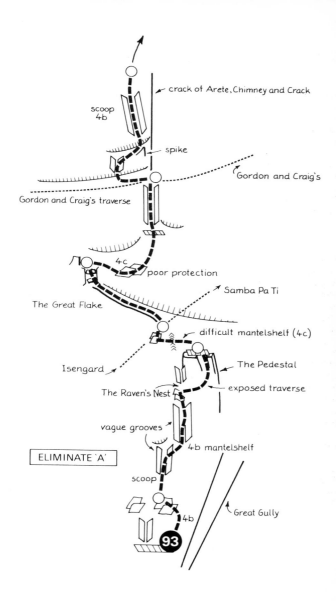

crack of Arete, Chimney and Crack

scoop
4b

spike

Gordon and Craig's

Gordon and Craig's traverse

4c

poor protection

Samba Pa Ti

The Great Flake

difficult mantelshelf (4c)

The Pedestal

Isengard

exposed traverse

The Raven's Nest

vague grooves

4b mantelshelf

ELIMINATE 'A'

scoop

4b

Great Gully

93

94: ISENGARD (E1) 55m / SAMBA PA TI (E2) 65m

Summary: In many ways a mis-matched pair: Isengard with its variety of problems of reasonable technicality, and Samba Pa Ti with its series of overhangs climbed on huge holds. Protection is good, but prusik loops should be carried by both leader and second.

First Ascent: Isengard – Les Brown and A.'Richard' McHardy, April 1962. Samba Pa Ti – Andy Hyslop and Rick Graham, August 1977.

Best Conditions: East facing at 700m. Allow three dry summer days.

Approach: Refer to the area introduction and crag diagram.

Starting Point: Start at the foot of a short and often greasy groove, just left of the start of Eliminate 'A' (Route 93) (or avoid by a detour to the left if wet).

Descent: Via South Rake (refer to Route 92).

The figure in red is spreadeagled in a seemingly impossible position, spellbound into place on an unbelievably impending wall. Overhangs to the fore. . . overhangs behind. . . did somebody mention the valley of death? The ropes loop down into a niche where an unseen second crouches, roof-low in fear. Crowds on the scree gawp in astonishment. Then suddenly that figure is you, and the blurs of distance focus into sharp edges of rock that provide the only available means of progress. Incredibly, it is possible to rest out there. Good runners and jugs abound and the nightmare turns to daydream. Even at the stance the ropes seem to defy gravity by hanging horizontally. But no, it really is that steep. Samba Pa Ti, one of the oddest route names in the district – according to Hyslop, a case of 'rock' inspiring rock.

Far below, and almost forgotten, lies Isengard – a direct start if you like. A peculiar scoop, a vicious crack requiring a long lurch, and an intimidating but surprisingly reasonable overhang, present themselves in logical sequence, like so many clues to be solved. It makes a reasonable E1 in its own right.

Together they make a formidable combination.

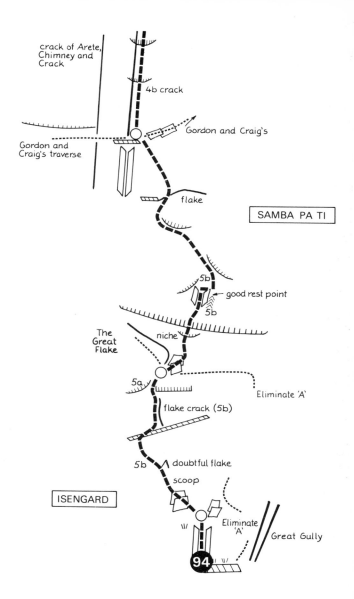

crack of Arete, Chimney and Crack

4b crack

Gordon and Craig's

Gordon and Craig's traverse

flake

SAMBA PA TI

5b

good rest point

5b

The Great Flake

niche

5a

Eliminate 'A'

flake crack (5b)

5b

doubtful flake

scoop

ISENGARD

Eliminate 'A'

Great Gully

94

95: GIANT'S CRAWL (D) 125m

Summary: One of the best Lakeland mountaineering routes, making an excellent way to the summit of Dow Crag prior to a walking tour of the Coniston Fells. Technical difficulty is only moderate, but good belays are hard to find on the great slab pitches – some flakes being very dubious – and the climb is unsuitable for complete novices due to poorly protected traverses. A selection of nuts should be taken.

First Ascent: Erik and Oscar Addyman, and Stobart, April 1909.

Best Conditions: East facing at 700m. Climbable at any time of year.

Approach: Refer to area introduction and crag diagram. From the mouth of Great Gully, which divides 'A' and 'B' Buttresses, a huge, right slanting gangway of a slab cuts across the upper section of 'B' Buttress, forming a parallel fault line to the lower Easy Way.

Starting Point: At the mouth of Great Gully, where a short scrambling pitch on the right gains the slab.

Descent: Continue to the summit and descend via South Rake (refer to Route 92).

Giant's Crawl is a giant zig-zag – the zig being the vast slab that carves a gigantic rightward-slanting swathe through the extreme territory of Upper 'B'. Hanging above Great Gully, this slab is exposed from the start, and becomes even more so about half-way up where it narrows and steepens simultaneously, squeezed from above and below into a slender gangway. Solo climbers often find themselves contemplating an overabundance of view at this point and scuttle back down muttering about family responsibilities.

Resolution or rope should let you reach the zag – a rising leftward line across the more broken upper part of the buttress. Mid-way again and a short nose-grinding crack demands varying amounts of struggle and clothing before landing leaders high and dry on a good platform. There is no way up from here, but an almost hands-in-pockets stroll to the left brings you back to the edge overlooking Great Gully. The view returns with a vengeance! You can tell yourself that the renewed trepidation has nothing to do with renewed difficulties, that it's just the exposure, that it's all in the mind. But it won't do any good. You'll still grip those holds in the final corner as if your life depended on it. Which it does.

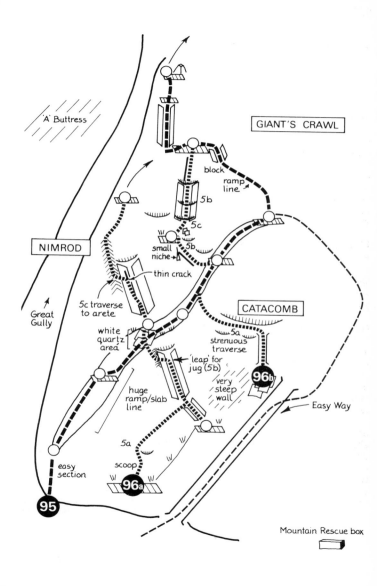

'A' Buttress

GIANT'S CRAWL

NIMROD

Great
Gully

block

ramp
line

5b

5c

small
niche

5b

thin crack

5c traverse
to arete

white
quartz
area

CATACOMB

5a
strenuous
traverse

'leap' for
jug (5b)

96b

very
steep
wall

Easy Way

huge
ramp/slab
line

5a

scoop

96a

95

easy
section

Mountain Rescue box

96: (a) Nimrod (E1) 100m
(b) Catacomb (E1+) 70m

Summary: A mindblowing pair of steep wall climbs. Technical difficulties are similar, but Catacomb is generally more strenuous. Good protection. Prusik loops should be carried on Catacomb. (Illustrated on Route 95 diagram.)

First Ascent: Nimrod – Dave Miller and Dave Kirby, June 1962; Catacomb – Rob and Murdoch Matheson, April 1972.

Best Conditions: East facing at 700m. Seepage can be a problem on both routes. Allow four dry days.

Approach: Refer to the area introduction and crag diagram.

Starting Point: The well-trodden break of Easy Way slants up from left to right across 'B' Buttress, effectively dividing it into two and providing a convenient means of descent. Both routes lie above Easy Way on the upper crag. Nimrod starts from a large grass ledge 5m directly above the start of Easy Way. For Catacomb, first scramble to the top of the initial chimney section of Easy Way and then go left over a mossy slab to start at the foot of a short vertical chimney below a roof.

Descent: Both routes finish on the upper section of Giant's Crawl which can be followed to the summit and a descent made via South Rake (as for Route 92). Alternatively reverse Giant's Crawl until a path can be followed on to the rake of Easy Way which is descended leftwards back to the starting point.

In the early 1960s the only 'nuts' around were Whitworth's. Drilled out and threaded on line, their potential had barely been realised at the time Nimrod was ascended. As a result, the second pitch was virtually unprotectable and a tension traverse was employed at the crux, many top climbers accepting aid of this sort as the only means of overcoming 'impossible' moves.

In the 1970s although the scene was set for change, Catacomb still marked the upper limit of free-climbing possibilities (though, in reality, it was little harder than its companion route of a decade earlier). Stupendously overhanging throughout, it has never been a climb to undertake lightly.

The following year, Austin's *Langdale* guide took a strong ethical stand. Even more important was the advent of proper wedge runners and a serious approach to training. Just three years later Livesey's ascent of *Footless Crow* showed everybody the shape of things to come.

Catacomb (Route 96b).
  (Climber: Ray Farragar. Photo: Stephen Reid.)

97: (a) Murray's Route (S) 80m
(b) Murray's Direct (VS) 55m

Summary: Marvellous climbing, typical of Dow. The long exposed traverse on Murray's is particularly spectacular.

First Ascent: Murray's – Dennis Murray, W.J. Borrowman and Brian Martin, April 1918. Direct Finish – Edgar Pryor and J.B. Meldrum, October 1922. Tiger Traverse – 'Dick' Mackereth, Bryan Tyson and Harry Griffin, September 1931. Link Pitch – Anthony Mullan, August 1945.

Best Conditions: East facing at 700m. Quick drying in summer, but likely to remain greasy in winter.

Approach: Refer to area introduction and crag diagram.

Starting Point: Under the centre of 'B' Buttress stands a blue Mountain Rescue box. Just left of this is a prominent V-groove. Murray's starts up the groove, whilst the Direct starts some 20m to the left at an embedded flake which gives access to a right-slanting gangway.

Descent: Follow the moderate rake of Easy Way down to the left.

In 1915, William Palmer, editor of the Fell and Rock Journal, lamented, 'Rock-climbing in the English Lake District has come to an end, except for soldiers and munition workers on furlough. . .' The records bear him out; during the war years the fells were virtually empty.

But by 1918 things were looking brighter, particularly for ex-prisoner-of-war Flt. Lt. Murray, who was able to reassess the obvious line on Dow both he and Herford had tried in happier days. His first forays were made with the intention of leaving the initial groove on the right, but, after falling to the ground on one attempt, he changed his line of attack to the unlikely-looking slab on the left. Crossing this involved a difficult change of feet with poor handholds and there was still an awkward bulge to come. Long run-outs were involved on every pitch and Borrowman thought the whole route 'exceptionally severe'.

Sections of the Direct were added over the following years. The Tiger Traverse inadvertently got its name when George Bower commented to Griffin that only a 'tiger' would get up it. It is a testing start, and the Link Pitch is by no means easy, but it is the compulsory lay-back of the Direct Finish that usually sorts out the sheep from the Goat's Water goats.

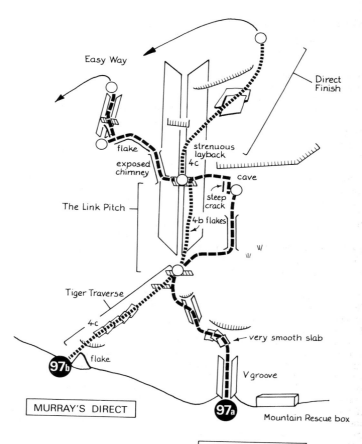

Easy Way

Direct Finish

flake

strenuous layback

4c

exposed chimney

cave

The Link Pitch

steep crack

4b flakes

Tiger Traverse

4c

very smooth slab

97b

flake

V groove

MURRAY'S DIRECT

97a

Mountain Rescue box

MURRAY'S ROUTE

98: (a) 'C' Ordinary (D) 110m
(b) Eliminate 'C' (VS+) 50m

Summary: Two excellent climbs with little in common apart from good rock. While the Ordinary Route is a much-ascended favourite the Eliminate quite rightly retains its well-earned reputation. (Illustrated on Route 99 diagram.)

First Ascent: 'C' Ordinary – George and A.J Woodhouse, August 1904. Eliminate 'C' – Bert Gross and George Basterfield, July 1922.

Best Conditions: East facing at 700m. Eliminate 'C' requires four dry days, whereas 'C' Ordinary is climbable in any conditions (although when wet it is much harder and more serious).

Approach: Refer to area introduction and crag diagram.

Starting Point: 'C' Ordinary starts just left of the lowest point of 'C' Buttress. For Eliminate 'C', follow Intermediate Gully (Route 99) to the first stance (or avoid this first pitch on the right at VD standard).

Descent: Traverse left on a narrow path under a steep wall. This soon leads to Easy Way, a moderate rake which is descended to the left.

The measure of these two climbs was summed up well in the first guide book to Dow. For whilst the Ordinary was graded 'Moderate; any number of patient climbers, who may smoke before, during, and after each pitch', the Eliminate was given 'very severe; rubbers; perfect conditions and morale.'

The Ordinary was the work of the Woodhouse Brothers, who visited the crag for a brief holiday and climbed the remarkable total of five new routes. Despite its ease, this is a highly satisfying and popular climb with a seemingly endless succession of cunningly turned problems on steep ground. Remarkably, for such a long climb, the standard is maintained throughout.

The Eliminate is a very different proposition. For a start, modern technology has done little to enhance the protection from that available in 1922. And as this was nil (apart from the stances), and given that the exposure is quite out of this world, it can be readily seen that a steady head, nerve and legs are desirable assets. This is particularly true of the final pitch, where all the action takes place on a hanging arête poised precariously above the gaping maw of Intermediate Gully.

Eliminate 'C' (Route 98b).
(Photo: Steve Ashton.)

99: INTERMEDIATE GULLY (S+) 70m

Summary: A splendid struggle involving much heave-ho and general hilarity. More difficult for short persons, especially if wet (the climb, that is). Helmets recommended.

First Ascent: Edward and John Hopkinson, April 1895.

Best Conditions: East facing at 700m. Climbable in any conditions but easier when dry. Allow five relatively rain-free days.

Approach: Refer to the area introduction and crag diagram.

Starting Point: The gully divides 'C' and 'D' Buttresses. Scramble up the easier lower section to the first steepening.

Descent: Immediately up on the left a narrow path under a steep wall leads on to Easy Way. Descend this moderate Rake leftwards. Alternatively, the line of the gully can be followed (care with loose rock) to the summit and the South Rake descent used (refer to Route 92).

There were five Hopkinson brothers, all highly talented in fields as diverse as medicine, commerce and law, and all good climbers. Edward was involved in the first ascent of Great Gully in 1888, and afterwards in the direct version. Nothing further was done on Dow until six years later, when a large party visited the crag with Intermediate at the top of their agenda. Lots were drawn and Edward and John won the prize, whilst Charles had to make do with the excellent Hopkinson's Crack.

Bower's description of Intermediate gives good warning of the rigours to come:

'There are members of the Club to whom "Intermediate" is more than a climb; rather is its ascent one of the solemn rites connected with the practice of a cult. To one such disciple did I write, asking for a description of the preparations necessary on the part of those who would attain to this circle. The reply came by wire: "Train on Raw meat and Stout, use Bulldog buttons. . ."

For the third pitch the leader should face inwards until the chockstone can be embraced, after which he faces right and uses back, knees and tongue. In wet weather there is an ominous cessation of the noise of running water during these operations.'

The penultimate pitch is generally acknowledged as the crux and though 'of guileless appearance exerts a curious influence on certain people. Staid and sober members of the club having been observed making desperate efforts to stand on their heads. . .'

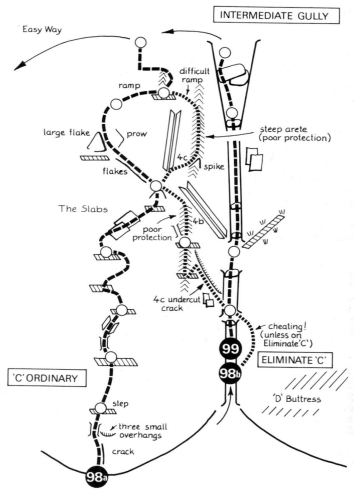

INTERMEDIATE GULLY

Easy Way

difficult ramp

ramp

large flake

prow

flakes

4c

spike

steep arete
(poor protection)

The Slabs

poor protection

4b

4c undercut crack

cheating!
(unless on Eliminate 'C')

'C' ORDINARY

ELIMINATE 'C'

99

98b

'D' Buttress

step

three small overhangs

crack

98a

* many variations possible on line shown *

100: (a) Great Central Route (HVS) 70m
(b) Hopkinson's Crack (S+) 50m

Summary: Both these climbs have an impact much greater than their length would suggest. The crux section of Great Central Route is very hard but it can be protected to some extent by a high side runner to the right.

First Ascent: Hopkinson's Crack – Charles Hopkinson and Otto Koecher, April 1895. Great Central Route – Joe Roper, George Bower, G. Jackson and A.P. Wilson, September 1919.

Best Conditions: East facing at 700m. Allow three dry days.

Approach: Refer to the area introduction and crag diagram. Easter Gully is between 'D' and 'E'

Buttresses. Climb it, passing the great chockstone on its left by the Cave Pitch (M), into the Amphitheatre.

Starting Point: At the back of the Amphitheatre is a large central buttress bounded by a pair of prominent wide cracks. Great Central Route starts between the cracks at the toe of the buttress, while Hopkinson's Crack follows the right-hand crack throughout.

Descent: A tenuous path leads more or less horizontally to the left, crossing Intermediate Gully, to join the Easy Way which is descended leftwards. From the top of Hopkinson's Crack, scramble up a bit to join this path.

'Think of a foothold; double it. Put your whole weight on it as you straighten out. Take away the hold you first thought of, and you will find yourself wondering how you got there.'

Had he lived to see it, Owen Glynne Jones might well have been describing the crux of Great Central Route, for footholds and handholds are there none, and for many years it was customary to steady the leader's boots on tiny wrinkles until he had located the vital ledge above. In fact, in the context of their times, high technical difficulty is a feature of both climbs. Hopkinson's Crack, a short but unrelenting route of impressive steepness, must have been a very bold lead indeed, given prevalent belaying methods.

Great Central Route, Hopkinson's Crack, Napes Needle, Central Buttress, and indeed every other route in this book, stand as monuments, not only to their discoverers, but also to that indomitable spirit of exploration and adventure that surely lives on in each subsequent ascent.

'Oh man, if only Lakeland could be left for each one of us exactly as he first knew it.' Lehmann Oppenheimer, *The Heart of Lakeland* (1908).

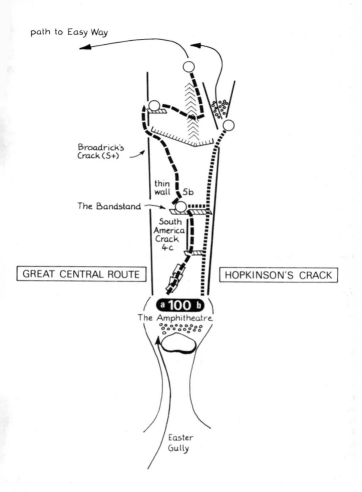

path to Easy Way

Broadrick's
Crack (S+)

thin
wall   5b

The Bandstand →

South
America
Crack
4c

GREAT CENTRAL ROUTE

HOPKINSON'S CRACK

a 100 b

The Amphitheatre

Easter
Gully

Also in the Crowood Classic Climbs series:

North Wales
Scotland – Central and Southern Highlands
Peak and Pennines

EMERGENCIES
First Aid Checklist

Check Breathing
- If necessary clear airway using a hooked finger to remove obstructions – vomit, blood, teeth etc.
- Turn casualty to lie in the recovery position (unless you suspect spinal injury). This helps to maintain a clear airway.

Check For Severe Bleeding
- Apply direct pressure from a pad to stop bleeding.
- Elevate the limb.

Check For Broken Bones
- Do not move the casualty if a spinal injury is suspected.
- Immobilise other fractures using improvised splints and slings.

Monitor Condition
- Keep casualty warm and comfortable while awaiting rescue (protect from wind and insulate from cold ground).
- Reassure casualty and monitor condition regularly.

To Alert Mountain Rescue
Dial 999, ask for police (mountain rescue), and try to have the following written details ready:
- Name and description of injured person.
- Precise location of injured person on crag.
- Location of crag (including *grid reference* and *map sheet* number).
- Time and nature of accident.
- Extent of injuries.
- Indication of prevailing weather at the scene (cloud base, wind strength, visibility, etc.).
- Remain by the phone until met by a police officer or member of the mountain rescue team.

Rescue Helicopters
- Secure all loose equipment before arrival of helicopter (weight rucksacks, jackets etc. with stones).
- Identify yourself by raising your arms in a V as helicopter approaches. Do not wave.
- Allow winchman to land of his own accord.
- Do not approach helicopter unless directed to do so by one of the crew (danger from rotors, exhaust, etc.).